YOUR LOVE DOES MATTER

YOUR LOVE DOES MATTER

A Journey to New Consciousness
and Expanding Your Love Footprint!

BY DAVID CUNNINGHAM

Published by Best Seller Publishing®, St. Augustine, FL
Best Seller Publishing® is a registered trademark.
Printed in the United States of America.

ISBN: 978-1966395454

For more information, please write:
Best Seller Publishing®
1775 US-1 #1070
St. Augustine, FL 32084
or call 1 (626) 765-9750

Visit us online at: www.BestSellerPublishing.org

DEDICATION

To humanity. I love you so very much.

May Love Prevail as the Preeminent
Way of Being on the Planet

Every human being who has the courage to probe deeply into the nature of truth will discover that love which is supreme knowledge.

—attributed to Albert Schweitzer

ACKNOWLEDGMENTS

To my beautiful husband, Bill: You are the greatest, most empowering husband in the whole world. You make everything I do worth it. And most importantly, you let me love you with all my heart and soul.

To my son, David Jr., my daughter-in-law, Janice, and my grandchildren, Garrett and Dawn: You even let me embarrass you and hug and kiss you in public! You are a miraculous gift to Billy and me. I love being your "Pops."

To my mom, Betty Andersen: I discovered myself in my relationship with you. With you I have discovered everything that matters to me and everything that is important to me.

To my dad: I wish your soul restful peace, and I am clear you lived the life you did so I could discover Love.

To my sister, Diane: You have always let me know you are proud of me, and now it is my turn to let the world know I am proud of you, my big sister!

To Werner Erhard: I have lived every minute of my life since 1983 in the clearing of your genius work, and I can only hope that I have assisted the delivery of your work to the world.

To Her Holiness Sai Maa: Every word I speak comes from the Self you awakened within me. Without You, my love was dormant and trapped. With You, my love is alive and vibrant and conscious.

To Chris Trammell: I *never* would have written this book without your guidance and encouragement. I had thought of writing a book for years and years … then you found me and told me to start writing. You were with me for every page, and you have opened every door that is allowing my life's work to get done *now*!

To Nancy Zapolski: From you I learned Grace, the most precious gift of all. The Grace you have bestowed on me lives on every page of this book.

To Laurel Scheaf: The man I am emerged with your leadership.

To all the Landmark Forum Leaders: As Jeff Wilmore once said, "We share the same blood."

To Ilene Muething: We have created so much together. Everything here in this book is a new expression of what we always envisioned; as Werner said, "A World that works for everyone, with no one left out."

To all Landmark Seminar Leaders: You made me believe we could indeed impact the whole world … and that Love Matters.

To Angie Mattingly: We never stop expanding (and laughing) together.

To Cindy and Henry, Josephine and Daphne Fischer: Living life with you has me think big, live big, and love big.

To Jo Fischer and Ryan Kiszka: I will never get over your wedding … the most beautiful wedding ever!

To Betsy and Marcel and Max Johnson: With your family, I found a most precious place in my heart, and that place is where I hold all of humanity today.

To Pontish Yeramyan: Your leadership has always had me be the committed human that I am.

To Chip Wilson: We really can accomplish anything, can't we?!

KIND WORDS FOR
YOUR *LOVE* DOES *MATTER*

Your *Love* Does *Matter* is our guidebook to resolving the most contentious conflicts of our time. Cunningham's gift to the world has left us able to see that when Love is where we come from, we are free to complete relationships that are not working, to embrace divergent points of view, to be with even our deepest fears, and to live a free and fulfilled life, finally! The book is all at once profoundly spiritual and extremely practical. A true gem.

—**SHEREEN DE PALMA**, FOUNDER/ATTORNEY,
HANNON DE PALMA & ASSOCIATES LLC

The emotional impact of this book is profound. It made me realize how love is not just a feeling but a force that can shape our lives and the world around us.

If you're ready for a transformative read that will inspire you to live more intentionally and love more deeply, I can't recommend Your *Love* Does *Matter* enough.

This book is for everyone—no matter where you are in life or what you believe, it will challenge you, uplift you, and invite you into new ways of living.

—**GALE BARNUM**, GLOBAL TRAINER, SPEAKER,
AND COMMUNICATION EXPERT

Your *Love* Does *Matter* is a heartfelt invitation to come home to your truest self—fully expressed, free, and alive. This isn't just another self-help book; it's a profound companion for your journey, deserving a place among the most impactful books you'll ever read. It transformed my being ... and my life, and if you open yourself to David's wisdom, it can transform yours too.

—**NADIA SARMOVA**, HOLLYWOOD PRODUCER

This book grounds us in the importance of acceptance and forgiveness and how fulfillment and happiness are always a choice.

—**MAURICE MITTS**, ESQUIRE

In the early years of my career, I studied the pioneers of science such as Charles Darwin, Alfred Russell Wallace, Edward Jenner, Harry Harlow, and numerous others. And in the latter half of my career, I engaged with the difference makers such as Wayne Dyer, Louise Hay, Marianne Williamson, Tony Robbins, and Deepak Chopra. And now, with this book, Your *Love* Does *Matter*, a new leader emerges: David Cunningham. His guidance and forward-thinking is revolutionary. What he proposes is as paradigm shifting as the great science leaders. And he is as gentle, loving, inspiring, and guiding as our modern healers and luminaries of consciousness and potential. For anyone who knows that their love is not being expressed or lived at the level of difference-making that it can be, then this book is the key to unlocking that new paradigm from within.

—**CHRIS TRAMMELL**, AUTHOR AND LIFE WORK ARCHITECT

The life-changing knowledge presented in Your *Love* Does *Matter* will lead you to discover your child-like ability to love again. You will learn techniques to recenter your soul to stay on the path of transformative love. It is magically beautiful, wonderful, insightful, vulnerable, and awesome to be able to access this level of awareness and love! Thank you, David, for your teaching, journey, commitment, and light!

—**MISSY WAINWRIGHT**, PHYSICIAN ASSISTANT
AND BEST MOM IN THE WORLD

Dear Reader, David Cunningham's book, Your *Love* Does *Matter*, is a gift to yourself. I have known David for more than 40 years, and I can tell you that he is one of the most special people in my life. One of the things I loved so much about the book is his personal stories, his journey to where he is today. A "must read."

—**AMY SPIELMAN**, COMMUNITY ADVOCATE

David's book is a gem. By sharing his own experiences with love in his life he created, for me, the world of love in my life that I hadn't really considered before. In doing so, his book provided me access to ways of being that have truly impacted the quality of my life. This book should be on the *New York Times* Bestseller list!

—**BRUCE SLOAN**, PHYSICIAN

FOREWORD
By
Nancy Zapolski, PhD
Clinical Psychologist

That my love mattered was an "of course" as I was growing up in a family that both showered love upon me and with open arms encouraged my full expression of love for them.

It startled me and broke my heart to realize that the whole world did not love the way we did.

The only question I had was, "How could I bring as much love to the world as possible?"

The career path I took was my best answer to that question.

And, in my over 40 years, both as a clinical psychologist and a leader of profoundly powerful worldwide transformational programs, I have been blessed with connecting with hundreds of thousands of people.

One of the things that all these people from all over the world have shown me over the years is that *all* of us have a profound desire to make a difference in life—to contribute and bring happiness to others.

The questions of "How do I do that?" and "What is my access to making a real difference with and for other people?" are shared questions.

This book answers those questions.

It is not what we do; nor is it what we have that allows us to make the difference we are out to make in the world.

It is our love! Our love is what makes the difference!

However, it is not always easy to live that way.

This book examines different elements that stop us from *living* our love—we are stopped by our judgments, our views, our beliefs, and what we know to be true, just to name a few.

And, most importantly, Your *Love* Does *Matter* gives us access to getting beyond and to the other side of all those stops.

*   *   *

At some point, given world events, I began to question if love was enough, however. In my heart, I knew love is exactly what is needed wherever there was conflict or suffering, and yet I doubted that *my* love and *my* loving made a big enough difference at all.

I knew I loved. That I loved was not at all in question.

But it made me sad to think that *it did not really matter* that I loved—that my love was insufficient or somehow insignificant.

Then, I read David's book!

Now, in my seventies, I am refreshed, full of hope, and as deeply committed as I ever was.

It is undebatable for me again, that every act of love, no matter how small … makes *all* the difference.

That I love … that you love … that we love is creating a dimension of love on this planet that all of us are living inside of together—as real as the physical atmosphere.

Yes, as David says, we have a **"Love Footprint,"** and I for one am paying attention to mine! And it makes me so happy to do so!

This book creates a pathway to new consciousness and is a literal guidebook to living as love in our families, in our communities, in our relationships, and in the world. It is clear, practical, and easy to follow.

It is revolutionary.

I invite you to more than read it … I invite you to let it touch your heart and impact your living.

A companion course to this book, Your
Love Does Matter, is available by scanning
the QR code below, or visiting the website
www.YourLoveDoesMatter.com

Your Love
Does Matter
Deepen your Work here.

SCAN
CODE

www.YourLoveDoesMatter.com

TABLE OF CONTENTS

Introduction 1

Section 1. Our Journey So Far

Chapter 1. Praying for Grace and Going Within.....................13
Chapter 2. Forgetting 21
Chapter 3. Wake-Up Calls I Slept Through 29

Section 2. Awakening New Consciousness

Chapter 4. Our Love Footprint: Establishing a Dimension
            of Love on the Planet..41
Chapter 5. Transformational Discoveries 45
Chapter 6. A Full Awakening...65
Chapter 7. I Am That I Am 69
Chapter 8. New Expressions 75
Chapter 9. Devotion..97
Chapter 10. Daily Affirmation: Sadhana 103
Chapter 11. Divine Love 107
Chapter 12. Knowing Yourself as Someone Who Bestows
            Grace on Another 111
Chapter 13. Daring to Love Source Openly and Unabashedly:
            The Joy of Sharing with Sai Maa 115

Chapter 14. Everywhere, All at Once, All the Time
(Loving Remotely) 121
Chapter 15. Honoring Our Word to Love 125
Chapter 16. Who We Are *Is* Love! 129
Chapter 17. The Point of Other People 131
Chapter 18. Freedom from Judgment 135
Chapter 19. Breaking from Source 139

Section 3. Living Today and Establishing a New Foundation for Living Tomorrow

Chapter 20. Acceptance 145
Chapter 21. Forgiving 149
Chapter 22. Betting It All on Your Love 157
Chapter 23. Love Goes to the Capitol 163
Chapter 24. Self-Love 167
Chapter 25. Fellow Travelers (Going First) 171

Afterword 175

INTRODUCTION

Dear Reader:

Your Love *Does* Matter. I am saying that directly to **you**, from the most precious place in my heart. Please hear me say to you, "Your love ... Yes, **YOUR** love, **DOES** matter."

This book, Your *Love* Does *Matter*, is written for new living. This book, Your *Love* Does *Matter*, is written for *the* new living that comes *only* with deeply knowing *who you really are* and *why you are here* ...

New living with joy;
>New Living as Your Highest Self;
>>New Living relating only to the Highest Self of others;
>>New Living as Source.

Most importantly, you will have a wholly new experience of yourself **as** the *loving being* you **are**, as you beautifully craft, like a piece of art, your ***Love Footprint*™**!

Some Books Must Be Written

Books such as Marianne Williamson's *Return to Love*, Wayne Dyer's *The Power of Intention*, Louise Hay's *You Can Heal Yourself*, and certainly the *Bhagavad Gita* gift us the opportunity to see, know, and experience ourselves with a new awareness of our ultimate creative power and a new awareness of our Source-full-ness.

These books each capture a possibility that leaves the reader aware, awake, in love with being alive, living with "conscious energy," and deeply moved by one's own existence … indeed, *Living in a State of Grace*.

These books transport the reader into a new kingdom: an eternal kingdom that is always there waiting to be discovered by all of humankind … a kingdom of enlightened existence and divinely inspired living "on earth as it is in heaven."

In the act of reading such a book, you enter this state of Grace.

This is one of those books.

You can read *about* leadership and not become a leader, can't you? You can read a book *about* being effective and not become effective. Yes?

This book is not *about* love; this book is a journey of love. This book is written as a journey we take together as fellow travelers, on a path to living consciously as love.

Together, we will:

- free ourselves from the beliefs that we are not already light, love, source
- shift to a new reality that who we are *is* light, love, source
- free ourselves from the obsolete, useless, and destructive paradigms of right and wrong, good and bad
- discover the nature of SELF as light
- discover the joy and power of "being" love, versus "having" love—the joy and power of bestowing Grace and *anchoring a dimension* of love on the planet
- start a movement, "The Love Matters Collaboration!"

Your *Love* Does *Matter* is written with profound love and deep respect for **you**. For over 50 years, I have been blessed to have my heart touched by the humanity of hundreds of thousands of people around the world. From what I have witnessed in hotel conference rooms, Fortune 100 boardrooms, in prisons and institutions, it is undeniable that when people are truly heard, healed, and freed from the hurts, resentments, regrets, and limiting views of their past—and when freedom is all there is—the *only thing* we want to express is **love** in its purest form.

And so it is that in this book, I will often address you as "My Beloved." And that is exactly who you are for me: My Beloved. Even if we have not met personally, you are fully My Beloved.

I love God.
   I love light.
      I love love.
         I love you.

Importantly, I invite you to *interact* with what is written here, versus merely *read* it. There is what is written here, and there is what happens for you while you read it. What happens for you intellectually, emotionally, and spiritually while you interact with what is written does start new living for you, gives you a new experience of being you, and provokes new and higher consciousness.

From time to time, I will offer a simple exercise to do. Each exercise is designed to heighten your awareness of your SELF and leave you living more and more consciously. Some of the exercises may be centering and meditative, while some of the exercises may evoke a new expression of your love. All of the exercises are designed to produce a new result for you in your home, work, or community life. If you find any exercise challenging, you may read on past it, but do come back to it when it feels right.

Let's try such a centering, meditative exercise now:

Be still

Sit without moving at all

Sit comfortably, with the spine as straight as it can be

Notice breathing

Do not try to manage breathing; simply notice breathing

Notice any elevation in your awareness

Welcome Being Aware

When ready, read the italicized lines below out loud, and visualize what is being said as you read.

While reading these lines you will be talking to your Soul. Your Soul will hear these words and be filled with the joy of being remembered by you.

Love is Eternal
Love is the Eternal Light that is never extinguished
Always, everywhere, all at once
Wrapping all that exists in its Golden White Glory
Pulsating in every atom, in every molecule and cell of the Universe
Love is the Eternal Om that is never silenced
Judging Nothing, Accepting All of Creation
My Soul is Home Here … Here in the Light, the Stillness, the Eternal Love,
The Forever Om
The Stillness is Love.
The Stillness is Me.
I am Stillness.
I am *the Stillness that tenderly embraces every particle of Creation …*
forever and always, since the very first moment.
Eternal, Infinite Love is Who **I Am**

Be still again
Breathe softly
Welcome the quiet stillness
Look around you, outside if you can
Be aware of the stillness, and as you are aware of the
stillness, say silently or out loud:

"There I am,
The Stillness is Me …
Yes, the Stillness is Me … Eternal, Infinite Love is Who I Am … I Am Love
I am the Love that wraps around the whole Earth and everything on the Earth."

The more something is said, the more it is affirmed, and the more real it becomes.

So please, repeat the declaration **"I *Am* Love"** 16 times, or as many times as you enjoy, or as many times as feels right for you. Repeating the declaration **"I *Am* Love"** 16 times begins to anchor the reality of the declaration for you. Why 16? In Eastern traditions, the number 8 and any multiple of the number 8 is associated with great expansion—I am calling upon the energy of the number 8 in making this recommendation. You can repeat this declaration anytime you think of it during the day. You can say it silently or out loud. Saying it out loud will have enhanced power.

Actually, anytime I invite you to repeat something out loud, standing in front of a mirror, looking yourself in the eye, will have the most power. Therefore, in this case, what will have the most power is saying **"I *Am* Love"** out loud to yourself in the mirror. If I was with you, I would take you by the hand and lead you to the mirror and ask you to look yourself in the eye and speak to yourself.

In the words of Eckhart Tolle:

"The eye with which I see God is the same eye through which God sees me. My eye and God's eye are one eye … One seeing, one knowing, one love."

Your honor of yourself, your love for yourself means everything to me.

Allow the new reality being created by saying **"I *Am* Love"** to become more and more potent for you each time you repeat it.

Yes, Who You are *IS* Love …
    Who You are *IS* Light …
        Who You are *IS* Source—fully and completely.

And we want to anchor this reality in your consciousness as you read this book.

Who You Are *Is* Love

You have not been educated that "Who You are *IS* Love," have you?

Okay, no problem … and it is important to acknowledge and embrace this fact.

It's been said, "One man's junk is another man's treasure."

Well, hopefully, one person's journey is another person's beaten path.

This book shares *my* journey of knowing,

> denying,
>> forgetting,
>>> working very hard …

and then coming face-to-face with divinity—coming face-to-face with my soul and its yearnings to love and coming face-to-face with a new consciousness.

Please let my journey serve you. It is a journey that has taken me around the world and allowed me to be with hundreds of thousands of human beings from all walks of life, from the celebrated to the marginalized to the institutionalized. This journey has taken me from being a young boy hiding in fear in his bedroom to being the leader standing in front of the room for hundreds and sometimes thousands of people at a time. This journey includes:

➤ Having grown up in a faithful, close-knit, loving family and then experiencing the anguish of that family turning brutally violent
➤ Having denied being gay, certainly to myself and everyone around me
➤ Having gotten married and becoming a father

➢ Having finally "come out of the closet," encountering the judgments of family and the world

➢ Having at age 32 been introduced to the genius transformational work of Werner Erhard, and then living the rest of my life to date out of what became possible by participating in his EST training in 1983

➢ Having spent an entire career in human services (i.e., starting as a special education teacher, serving as a director of both the Connecticut Justice for Children Collaboration and the National Committee for Prevention of Child Abuse, and then leading transformational programs for hundreds of thousands of people around the world for 35 years)

➢ Having finally been introduced to the Guru (spiritual teacher), Her Holiness Jagadguru Sai Maa, and being awakened to a new consciousness and being freed, truly freed to love fully and express all that was within my heart and soul ... with no hesitation, doubt, embarrassment, or shame

➢ Having resolved for myself that the most powerful question I could keep in front of me at all times is, "How do I give the most life to the most people—as fast as I can?!"

I am sharing this journey of liberation from the *illusion of separation from Source* and liberation from the *lack of knowing the SELF that dwells within*, to the remembrance of *who I really am* (we really are) as love, light, and source itself.

While the circumstances of your life may look nothing like mine, the purpose of this book is to find you wherever you are, having had your very own life experiences, and open the door for you to live as Grace and in Grace ... and to accompany you as you step through that door of new consciousness.

Your *Love* Does *Matter* is presented in three sections:

I. "Our Journey So Far" – In this section, we will explore how we have come to be the loving beings we are today—how we ended up "here," loving the way we love.

II. "Awakening New Consciousness" – In this section, we will discover together radical, revolutionary new paradigms of Being and Loving that immediately open the door for relating to ourselves and others in new ways. This is the largest section of the book. Much new learning is available here.

III. "Living Today and Establishing a New Foundation for Living Tomorrow" – In this section, we will create new pathways for consciously expanding our **Love Footprint** in our personal lives and in society.

I want this book to make sense to you, and I want each step along this journey to be clear for you. But at the same time, I want you to *experience* what is written here, not merely read and understand it.

So now, my Beloveds, before we go on, I want to give you the opportunity to recenter yourself. This will demonstrate that you can serve yourSELF in this way anytime, anywhere, several times a day if you wish. This book is here as a guide to your journey. You can read from it, do the recommended exercises, and visit www.yourlovedoesmatter.com. All is dedicated to your journey.

Please pause a moment and begin a new exercise.

Take a breath, and say to yourself again, **"I am light, I am love, I am source"** 16 times.

Say it out loud.

Your eyes can be open or closed. Again, repeating **"I am light, I am love, I am source"** serves to anchor that reality in your consciousness.

As you read this book, the light and love and healing consciousness that is already and always there in the cells of your body will be activated and enlivened with new energy. Be open to experiencing a vibrant energy in the cells of your body. Take your time. Bring to your mind's eye the cells of your body, the various organs, and the strands of DNA. Take your time. Imagine every cell of you glimmering with light and rejoicing in being fully and totally loved.

I love you.

I had to write this book. My Soul demanded it.

Listen for what your soul is asking for … it will tell you.

If your soul is wanting love, love for you and love for all beings, then

> Come, come with me, my Beloved,
> Let us be fellow travelers.
> Let me accompany you to this state of GRACE.

Together, we will be fulfilled in discovering **YOUR *LOVE* DOES MATTER!**

- ★ **YOUR LOVE MATTERS TO YOU!**
- ★ **YOUR LOVE MATTERS TO ANYONE WHO CROSSES YOUR PATH—FOR A MOMENT OR FOR 50 YEARS!**
- ★ **YOUR LOVE MATTERS FOR MOTHER EARTH AND ALL OF HUMANITY!**

It is both simple and profound. I am inviting you to live the life of someone who knows and says, "My Love Does Matter—It Matters that I Love!"

When you are ready, begin Chapter 1.

Section 1

Our Journey So Far

Chapter 1

Praying for Grace and Going Within

It's not in the stars to hold our destiny but ourselves.
—William Shakespeare

Very recently I had a remembrance. A remembrance is the experience of remembering something from a different dimension of existence.

My remembrance is this:

Just before I was born ... I did not want to be born. I am arguing with God.

I am adamant: "I WON'T GO UNLESS I CAN HEAL PEOPLE'S SUFFERING!"

"IF YOU GIVE ME THE POWER TO LOVE AND HEAL, I WILL GO."

God's answer is, "YES, YOU HAVE THE POWER TO LOVE AND THE POWER TO HEAL,"

and so I am born.

My Beloved, have you wondered what contract you may have for this lifetime?

Let yourself wonder. Just wondering about it is enlivening. Wondering opens us up to what inspires us and what is possible that we have never imagined before. Wonder, now, what could your contract for this lifetime be?

A remembrance may come to you right away or after a while— no matter when, your consciousness will have been awakened simply by the wondering. Wondering is a very high state of consciousness. You can practice wondering as often as you like, alone or with others.

The Velvet Painting

The first time I experienced myself as having a contract with God was when I was four years old. I was taken to church for an evening candlelight service. Our church was a tiny, wood-frame evangelical church in the small town of Olean in western New York State.

The church I first experienced Christ's Love,
Olean Showers United Methodist Church.

I had never seen anything so beautiful. The sanctuary was lit only by candles. I leaned against my mom. She was wearing her old fur coat, old and moth eaten but a source of elegance and pride for my mom. Her wearing that coat that evening indicated how special this event was.

The entire service was dedicated to watching an artist paint on a black velvet canvas. In beautiful colors on this black velvet, the artist was painting Christ laying His hands on children and healing the children with His loving touch.

It was the most beautiful painting this four-year-old had ever seen!

At that moment, I knew love and I knew I loved. I knew, as an eternal truth, knowing that I loved humanity just as Christ loved humanity. I was so deeply happy. I believe it was my first conscious experience of my soul.

Then, over time, a fog of forgetfulness set in, and for many years I forgot! I forgot that my love was as strong as Christ's love.

I forgot that I loved humanity so much that *my love* could heal people's suffering.

Therefore, for many years, having forgotten the contract I made with God, I longed in my heart to be able to heal anyone who was suffering, as if I were not already and always capable.

Forgetting my contract was so deadening over the decades.

Until, now at age 72, having met and been blessed by Jagadguru Sai Maa, I remember!

I REMEMBER I LOVE
I REMEMBER I LOVE TO LOVE
I REMEMBER I LOVE LOVE!

Overwhelmed with gratitude in the grace of the Jagadguru, I went within, I prayed, and my soul wrote:

"PRAYER OF GRACE"

May I Use These Arms to Hold the Whole World Tenderly

May I Use These Hands to Heal All Who Suffer

May I Use These Eyes to See the Divine Within All People

May I Use These Ears to Listen for the Truth

May I Use This Mind to Think of Us as Light Beings

May I Use This Mouth to Create Possibility, Remembrance, Awareness, Devotion, and Creation Itself

May I Use These Feet to Walk in the World and Bestow Grace on All

May I Use This Heart to Love Without Conditions

May I Use This Whole Being to Anchor the Dimension of Love on This Planet

I invite you to pause, be still and quiet, and pray this prayer as *your* prayer. Pray it with me now and claim it as your prayer. Take this prayer, my Beloved; I give it to you. It is yours as it is mine.

Now breathe and rest. Rest in the stillness this prayer brings you. Close your eyes and look inward. See the *You* that you only see when you look inward, not outward.

Notice what verse of the prayer spoke to you the most. Did you have a favorite verse? Then ask yourself, "Who must I be if that verse is my soul's favorite verse?"

This book is written with great, great love for you.

I hold you in my embrace as I write every word. I am holding you right now, my Beloved.

Experience being wrapped in love right now.

Love is there, surrounding you. Can you feel it?

Close your eyes and get present to the cells of your body. Can you experience the love that is pulsating within each cell of your body? That pulsating love is the infinite boundless love of Source for all of creation.

And at the same time, that is *your* love for ALL OF HUMANITY.

➢ Enjoy being loved.
➢ Enjoy loving.
➢ Love loves love.

Before you read further, let's practice together "**GOING WITHIN**."

Note: If you prefer a guided meditation, you can use the link provided.

> [Please visit www.YourLoveDoesMatter.com and the guided meditation created in the companion course.]

Find a quiet place to sit.

Notice your breathing.

Do not try to change your breathing. Simply notice the inhale and the exhale.

Be as still as possible. Be in a comfortable position with the spine as straight as it can be.

And breathe.

Breathe.

After a few breaths, with the eyes closed, intentionally pause between inhaling and exhaling (for at least a count of 4).

Repeat at least five times, intentionally pause between inhaling and exhaling (for at least a count of 4).

Discover the nothingness that lives there, *between* the inhale and the exhale.

It is a space, an infinite space.
It is nothing. And in its boundlessness, it is everything.
Between the inhale and the exhale, rest for a moment.
Enjoy that space. It is peaceful there.
It is the space of perfection.
It is the space of Source. It is the space of Creation.
Everything is, and always has been, created in and from this nothingness.
Source is all that is.

Fall in love with this divine space. It is always there, just between the inhale and the exhale, waiting for you to be aware of it. YES, LOVE THE LOVE.

Now shift the attention to the heart area. Be aware of what is there. There is a consciousness there. Bring your awareness to the consciousness in the heart area. Rest in it. Keep breathing. This consciousness loves. This consciousness loves you. This consciousness loves all beings. This consciousness loves all of existence.

This is the consciousness of the Divine Feminine that is always, always there, waiting for us to be aware of it. Spend time there. Fall in love with this consciousness.

And now think to yourself, "This consciousness is me! I am the consciousness. This consciousness is who I AM!" Enjoy being this perfect love consciousness. Enjoy being this source of Grace.

Be aware; stay in this stillness as long as you enjoy.

This is your *natural* state. The other states of anxiety, guilt, indifference, righteousness, and resentment have become "normal"—but "normal" and "natural" are not the same.

Grace is your *natural* state.

Go within; Grace is always there waiting for you to come live in Her.

Jagadguru Sai Maa

At different times in the book, I will refer to Her Holiness Jagadguru Sai Maa. Do not worry if you have no knowledge of what a Guru is or even if you have no interest in knowing a Guru. Being related to a Guru has been part of my journey; it may or may not be part of yours.

My Beloved, this book is about love and not about spirituality. Some may have no interest in pursuing a spiritual path, but *everyone* deals with loving. I will share with you how my spiritual awakening brightened my love and my loving. If you would like to learn more about Sai Maa, I encourage you to visit www.awakenedlife.love.

I have chosen Sai Maa as my Guru and acknowledge Sai Maa as the source of my full awakening. In my experience, Sai Maa is accompanying me every step along the way on my path to enlightenment.

In fact, I recently had a minor stroke. Sai Maa immediately responded with love and suggested health interventions, from rest and diet to stem cell therapy. Sai Maa was in daily communication with either me or my husband. And more than that, I could feel Divine Feminine Energy throughout my body, in the cells of my body.

I have emerged from this experience with a renewed awareness of purpose. The Grace I have received awakened anew my soul's yearning to love fully.

This deep connection to Divine Consciousness moves me and touches my heart.

This deep connection to Divine Consciousness awakens the love within me.

Yes, I would assert that Divine Consciousness greatly deepens our awareness of SELF as LOVE.

And for all of us, Sai Maa is at work anchoring a *dimension of love* on the planet. Imagine there is a new energetic field of Divine Feminine Consciousness being established.

Imagine that this consciousness exists as love in every molecule of existence, and that it has been dormant but could be active. Sai Maa is activating that love. Sai Maa activates the love in the cells of our body, our heart, our lungs. Every experience I have had being with Sai Maa has been wonderfully enlivening.

Can you imagine going from a smoke-filled room into a room with clean air? Instantly, you could breathe easier, couldn't you? Imagine yourself not only loving but also living in an environment of love. As humanity moves from the fear-filled field it has been in for centuries to a love-filled field, don't you think something wonderful could happen for us?

Chapter 2

FORGETTING

Love is the ultimate truth at the heart of the
universe and transcends all boundaries.
—Deepak Chopra

I now remember forgetting. I now remember forgetting how deeply I love, forgetting that my love matters, and forgetting that who I am *is* Love.

Please use my memories of forgetting to remember the times in your own life where you forgot how deeply you love, when you forgot that your love does matter, and when you forgot that who you are *is* Love. My Beloved, I invite you to pause occasionally while reading and ask yourself the questions, "What do I remember?" and "What happened in my life that had me question, or had me forget that it mattered that I love?" Bringing those memories forward in your consciousness will give you the opportunity to reclaim the depth and power of your loving today.

Moments of Forgetting "My Love Does Matter"

I was five years old, in Sunday school, at the same church where I experienced the boundless love of Christ in my heart. I was told I was a sinner.

On one of those little felt boards with vinyl cutouts that stick to it, my Sunday school teacher put a white heart and a black heart. She proclaimed that good people have white hearts and sinners have black hearts. Then she proclaimed, "And you all have black hearts!"

My hope of living in the example of Christ was over; I was, said my teacher, a "sinner."

*   *   *

When I was seven years old, my immediate family (i.e., Mom, Dad, and sister Diane) left everyone else to move from rural northwestern Pennsylvania to La Porte, Indiana. *Nobody* had ever left "home" before. "Home" was Eldred, Pennsylvania (with a population of only 760 persons in 2020 and much fewer in 1958).

As we drove away, I was looking out the back window of our car and watched my Grandma Vaughn collapse on the ground, hysterically crying at our leaving. I looked to the front seat at my parents to see what they were going to do; I could not believe that we just continued driving away.

I couldn't imagine that it did not matter how upset everyone was, that our love did not matter. We were just driving away while Grandma wept.

*   *   *

When I was around eight, my dad started beating my mom mercilessly. It continued for years. I remember standing at the top of the stairs in the kitchen looking down to the TV room and seeing my dad hit my mom so hard she fell to the floor. I screamed for him to stop and was told coldly to go to bed. I laid in bed with a pillow over my head but could not block out the sound of my dad's fist pounding my mom. This is my mom and dad, and we were supposed to love each other. Love did not matter.

*　　*　　*

When I was 13, we moved again, this time from Indiana to Connecticut. My sister was a senior in high school, and we were moving in December, meaning she would not finish her senior year. She was devastated *and* she was in love with her boyfriend, Jaime. She begged my parents to let her stay with her friend Claudia and finish her senior year *or* let her marry Jaime.

She was truly heartbroken. My parents firmly said no, she had to move with us.

We moved, Diane finished high school by getting a GED, and went to work as a bank teller. Once again, love did not matter. There were some rules that my parents lived by that ignored our hearts.

*　　*　　*

My Grandfather Cunningham was visiting us in Connecticut. He and my grandmother still lived in Olean, New York, right across the state line from Eldred. He got up from the dinner table, went out in the backyard, collapsed, and died from a heart attack. He had been sitting right there beside me moments earlier. If I had known that he was about to die, I would have held him and poured my love out to him. But I hadn't, and he was dead.

We shipped Grandpa's body back to Olean. We all got in the car and drove my grandmother home for the funeral. In the back seat, for that eight-hour ride, sitting silently next to my grandmother, watching her be so stoic and not understanding the depths of their relationship, I felt foolish for feeling so sad.

*   *   *

Both my grandmothers were widows now, living alone and obviously lonely. I could not understand why we did not have them come live with us … only to conclude again that our love did not matter.

*   *   *

I started being aware of being gay when I was about 10.

Certainly, when I was 15 and had my friend Rob for a sleepover, I was desperate to touch him and be touched. I ever so slightly brushed his leg with my hand, and he said, "Stop that!" I withdrew my hand quickly. My love was forbidden.

And around that time, Anita Bryant, Jerry Falwell, and the Pope all took to the world stage to say my love was disgusting and forbidden.

*   *   *

I dated women, I got married at age 22, and we had our son when I was 25. And the whole time something was terribly missing. I would have secret gay encounters, hate myself afterward, and promise myself I would never do so again.

I never saw a man more than once. It was all forbidden love.

*   *   *

In 1976, my good friend and colleague Sam was the subject of a "fag bashing" on the streets of Hartford, Connecticut. Sam was a dedicated social worker and child and family advocate. Sam was lovingly raising two foster sons. None of that mattered. They beat him with a baseball bat. Righteous bigotry mattered to them, not love.

*   *   *

When my first husband, Hayden, was dying of AIDS in 1987, the things that were shouted at us, espoused on TV, or whispered behind our backs were devastating. We loved each other. He was a brilliant, 29-year-old vibrant human being. None of that mattered to so many people. "This is God's punishment," we were told. God is punishing us for our love? Really?

*   *   *

When the COVID epidemic started, I led a Zoom call for about 500 people to offer support and community. I expressed my love for the people on the call, and the next day a colleague told me that it was "disgusting."

*   *   *

In 2021, I started to participate in a local church. It was familiar and comforting in one way, singing familiar hymns and reciting the Lord's Prayer. But then I found out the entire church, worldwide, was voting on whether or not to allow gay ministers and whether or not to allow any of their ministers to perform gay marriages!

My love was being *voted on*, worldwide, as acceptable or not?!

No matter how the vote turns out, isn't the assumption trouble-some that some love is valid and other love is not valid and is to be voted on? People are still voting on one another?!

*　　*　　*

MY BELOVED: Have you forgotten too? Have you forgotten how much you love? Have you forgotten that you ARE love? Have you forgotten that the love you are is boundless, eternal, and infinite?

Have you forgotten that your love does MATTER? By the end of this book, I want you to *love your love* again.

So take the time now to remember when you forgot how much you love to love. If you want to, write down these memories for yourself. I recommend you note the year the event took place, your age, and then a brief description of the event.

When did you forget the infinite love you are? What happened in your life where you forgot how much your love does matter?

As you remember these times, you want to be careful to neither regret having forgotten nor criticize yourself or anyone else for your forgetting. It takes courage to be aware that you have forgotten, and the remembering process itself activates the love that has been dormant in each cell of the body.

It is not the case that you ever stopped loving. Love, your love, is eternal. It is the case that you forgot you love.

We do become preoccupied with other energies—righteousness, judgment, defensiveness, self-justification, worry, doubt, and so on. These energies are like clouds that may temporarily block the sun, but they never, ever extinguish the sun.

Yes, your love is eternal in the same way the sun is eternal. Your love may sometimes be out of our consciousness, yet it is always there, patiently and devotedly waiting for the clouds to pass.

So let the clouds come to your awareness so that you know they are not everything.

There is light behind the clouds. Please, please start identifying yourself as the eternal light—the eternal light is you. You exist before the clouds come and after they pass. Let them pass. As you begin to identify yourself as the eternal light, you will begin to love yourself as I love you.

I love you as I do because I know who you really are. As we travel together, you will come to love yourself as I love you. Then, as you discover who you really are, you will wake up to who others are and love all others as you love yourSELF—why would you not? They are eternal light; you love light—why would you not be madly in love with all beings?

Chapter 3

WAKE-UP CALLS I
SLEPT THROUGH

Where there is love there is life.
—Mahatma Gandhi

There were wake-up calls (i.e., life events where LOVE tri-umphed). Allow me now to share with you several moments in my life where I experienced deep love.

I did experience these moments of deep love. However, they were all experienced inside of a context that my love *did not* matter, and, in fact, my love was disgusting, if not forbidden.

So these moments never added up. They in fact, ultimately, were invalidated. No matter what, I for myself still had no right to love. And if I did love, it could only be the emotions and experiences of a "sinner" or a "sissy."

So I slept through these wake-up calls. I experienced them, but I did not wake up and remember that *My* Love Does Matter.

As you read my moments of great love, let your own memories come to you. When have you experienced deep love? I am sure you have. Whether in a journal or in the margins of this page, I invite you to take some notes so you can explore your memories fully after you are done reading this chapter.

Moments of Great Love

In 1971, I had a crush on a girl named Sally. Sally did not want to go out with me, but she told me she was volunteering at a state facility for children with mental disabilities and invited me to go with her. I went just to be with her.

We walked into the facility and found about 30 severely disabled children lying on the floor, mostly screaming. I was horrified and backed up against the wall. I had never seen anything like this. I did not know facilities like this existed or that any child anywhere lived such an existence.

Sally was so brilliant. She scooped up a little girl named Diane. Diane was deaf, dumb, blind, profoundly intellectually disabled, and seriously self-mutilating. Diane would hit herself and poke her own eyes. The theory was that she hit herself and poked her eyes because it was the only sensory stimulation she got.

Sally scooped Diane up and put Diane in my arms, and I melted. The tears started rolling down my cheeks. I felt a love and compassion stronger than I had ever had for any human being. I was so alive. Alive with love.

*   *   *

When I began having gay encounters, I refused to see a man more than once—and then I met Tony. After our first encounter, Tony found me and called me the next day at work. I couldn't believe he had found me; I was terrified at being "outed."

But Tony gently said he simply wanted to see me again. I said yes, then a third time, then a fourth time, and many thereafter. One time we were together and I experienced something I had never experienced before and did not know was possible ... I was fully *in love* with Tony!

I could not believe it. I could be *in love* with a man! I was not broken after all. I can be in love! I do love!

My experience was so profound, I felt as though I would die if I forbid myself from this love for another man. Of course I would not have died, and yet it did seem so. **I HAD NOT EVER FELT LOVE LIKE THIS BEFORE.**

*   *   *

In 1983, I was at a meeting where there were several opportunities presented to be a volunteer. There were several breakout rooms with various leaders presenting different volunteer opportunities. I was quite intimidated and did not have a clue where I should go. I walked down the hallway and stood outside different doorways, listening for a few minutes to the different presenters. Everything was ordinary until I stood outside one doorway and the hairs on the back of my neck literally stood up. Whoever was speaking was alive and vibrant and inspired and visionary. It was no less than listening to Jesus, Dr. King, or Gandhi speak.

I did not dare go into the room. I waited outside until the presentation was over, and others filed out of the room. Then I peeked in to see who was this person who was so connected to God, whose words were awakening my Soul.

There was this young, strikingly handsome Black man whose eyes and voice were riveting. I did not meet him that evening, nor did I learn his name.

A few months later, I started a six-month high-level training program to be a leader at this same organization. The first night, as I sat and waited for the program to begin, I lost my breath when this same young Black man walked in, introduced himself as Hayden, and announced he would be leading our program.

Hayden, age 24, at our wedding.

As the six months passed, I fell deeply in love with Hayden.

At the end of the program, I moved to Manhattan to be with him, to be his soulmate for life. My soul yearned to be his partner in life, in every way. I was as alive and in love beyond anything I had ever imagined.

* * *

In 1988, the doctors told me that Hayden was dying. He was 28 years old.

I was at a loss. I quit my job. Hayden was dying of AIDS. I was sitting in the hospital room in San Francisco, wondering what in the world I could do. Deanna and Jonathon (friends of Hayden's whom I had never met) walked in the room, introduced themselves to me, and simply asked, "What do you need?"

I told them I had no place to take Hayden. They miraculously offered that they had a small house on the property where they lived on Long Island, in New York. The house was unoccupied, and with boundless love and generosity, Deanna and Jonathon, whom I had met only five minutes earlier, invited me to bring Hayden there. I cried in the presence of this generosity of strangers. This is where Hayden died a few months later, and Jon and Deanna were with me as Hayden took his last breath.

*   *   *

For the move to New York, I called a limo company, and told them I needed a driver who would pick Hayden and me up at the hospital. I needed a driver who would help place Hayden in the car. I needed a driver who would go with me to the gate at the airport and help me board Hayden on the plane. I was so afraid that they would send someone uncaring or someone afraid of AIDS and touching Hayden.

They sent an angel.

This driver came and with so much respect and compassion, he gently lifted Hayden into the car and then carried Hayden from the car into the airport until we secured a wheelchair. The driver stayed with us every moment until we were safely boarded. I again cried at the kindness of a stranger.

*　　*　　*

In 1988, the AIDS quilt was spread out on the Washington Mall.[1] I had made a patch for Hayden. (Ultimately, the quilt included 48,000 patches, weighed 54 tons, and spanned 1.2 million square feet.)

Deanna and Jon drove my sister and me to Washington, DC to submit Hayden's patch to be included in the quilt.

The process of submitting Hayden's patch was emotional, like turning over my heart to a stranger. But the volunteers were so compassionate, and it went smoothly. Then we walked out onto the Washington Mall, surrounded by acres and acres of the quilt, with white cloth pathways allowing visitors to walk among and see all the patches, among hundreds of volunteers all dressed in white, reverently quiet, gently guiding, and tenderly comforting. As if angels were walking among us—this must be what it is to be in the valley of the siddhas.

[1]　The AIDS Quilt was conceived in November of 1985 by human rights activist Cleave Jones. The goal was to create a memorial of those who had died of AIDS and help people understand the devastating impact of the disease.

*　　*　　*

In 1994, I met Bill, whom I have now been with for 30 years. I could not believe I was going to have the opportunity to be in love again. Bill is the most generous and kind "family man" I have ever met in real life. He is the perfect middle child of nine.

Bill and I the day we were legally married, September 13, 2014.

*　　*　　*

When the World Trade Center was attacked in 2001, I was in Tel Aviv leading a program for 200–300 people. As I learned the news, first I was terrified. My company's offices were in the World Trade Center—had we lost any of our people? As I learned all were safe, my fear turned to extreme sorrow for all the lives lost. I was in front of the room, leading the program as I wept. We all wept, and as we shared our common grief, our souls connected and deep, deep love—indeed, a profound communion—arose. We went out onto the streets of Tel Aviv and joined in the reverent vigil with thousands. Grief is an expression of love, isn't it? We shared grief, we shared an absolutely profound love.

*   *   *

Between 2005 and 2008, my son dropped out of communication with me. I texted, I called, I tried to reach him through his mom. He was living in Connecticut, and I was living in the Philadelphia area.

Nothing … complete radio silence.

Finally, I told Bill I was going to drive to my son's house and park in the driveway until he came home. I didn't care if it took a month. I would just sit there and wait for my son. Bill went with me. We arrived literally two minutes after my son had gotten home himself. What grace!

I knocked on the door. David said, "What are you doing here?" I replied, "I came to find my son." He burst into tears. Love mattered.

*   *   *

I was walking through the slums of Mumbai. Even if it is midday, the alley is dark, crammed between the buildings that serve as sweatshops during the day and living quarters at night. The stench is inescapable. The heat is suffocating. In the dark, I trip over something. I turned to look back for what I had tripped on. To my horror, it was a little girl, probably six years old, whom I had not seen sitting in the alley. I went back to her. With a huge smile, she held up a paper for me to see. It was an arithmetic work paper of addition problems. She was so proud. I smiled back and clapped for her. She held the paper to her heart and sat there beaming, in the heat, in the dark, in the filth. Love mattered.

I will never forget her.

*   *   *

I was particularly discouraged one day, feeling disconnected from my colleagues and unwanted in my organization. One colleague (Randy) called me and offered me Grace. Randy tenderly explained that no matter what, God loved me (substitute whatever language connects for you—e.g., Source, Allah) and that God's love: (a) did not have to be deserved, and (b) would never be taken away.

This kind of love is Grace, Randy explained. Randy invited me to live in Grace, and right there in that moment, I discovered Grace as a presence.

Ever since then, I have been devoted to Grace for humankind, and right now that means you, dear Reader. I wish you Grace. I bet you are devoted to Grace for humankind too! Would you love it if the world lived in a state of Grace?

*   *   *

In 2014, Bill and I were able to be legally married. My son was our best man, and his toast included the sentiment, "My dad taught me how to love."

*   *   *

So here I am, 72 years of age, having spent a lifetime loving deeply, having experienced the deepest love and the deepest grief, and having been utterly convinced my loving did not matter or—worse—was a sin and disgusting.

My Beloved: Our love *does* matter. **Your** love does matter. Wherever you are in your life journey, I pray to awaken the love within you and have you share your love fully and experience the true joy of being alive.

Especially to men: I have listened to many men say that for whatever reason, they do not express their love. If you are a man reading this book, it does matter that you share your love. Please.

Have you also slept through wake-up calls where you have been deeply moved by love, by grief, by life events where LOVE triumphed?

Wake up with me now.

Our love does matter.

I am inviting you to bet everything on your love. Rather than relying on your logic, your knowledge, or your personality to get what you want in life, what if you relied first and foremost on your love (i.e., the love that you are)?

Section 2

Awakening New Consciousness

Chapter 4

OUR LOVE FOOTPRINT: ESTABLISHING A DIMENSION OF LOVE ON THE PLANET

*Love has nothing to do with what you are expecting
to get—only with what you are expecting to give—which
is everything.*
—Katharine Hepburn

Imagine you just interacted with a clerk in a store for a minute. Ask yourself: Do they feel better about themselves or worse about themselves after the minute they spent interacting with you? Are they more inspired or less inspired with their job? Is love present; can you feel it? What is left behind when you leave this interaction?

You have lunch at your family house, and your siblings and their spouses are all there. Is everyone around the table moved in the presence of your love for them and their love for one another? If we replayed everything you said during your time together and listened for love being expressed, would we hear it?

Or would we hear judgment, opinion, and debate? What is left behind when you leave the gathering?

You traveled on an airplane. You boarded, stowed luggage, took your seat, gathered your luggage, and deplaned. As you left the plane, what was the experience of the flight crew? As you left the plane, what was the experience of your fellow passengers? Did they experience love from you? Or was it indifference? Or was it even righteousness?

You have been married 25 years. What is your spouse's ultimate experience? Do they feel bigger and more complete as a human being having spent 25 years with you? Are they present to be loved? Do they experience their love of you being welcomed?

Pretend it is 5 p.m. and you have been awake and interacting with people for about 10 hours so far this day. Look back on every interaction and put it in a category based on what was present during the interaction. Was it love, or was it indifference, resentment, judgment, fear, impatience, criticism, false platitudes, or defensiveness? What percentage was love, really?

Look back on your life to date. Can you be honest with yourself and say if the world has more love or less love in it because you walked the earth for as long as you have?

Yes, imagine we not only have a carbon footprint, but we also have a **Love Footprint** that is real! What if each of us were conscious of our **Love Footprint**, honest about our inventory, and consciously causing the presence of love to expand by virtue of our living? What kind of society would that be? Would you like to cause that together? What if we all took this seriously?

I invite you to take your personal inventory now. What would you want to see?

What do you see?

How would you rank your last interaction with another person on the following scale of 1 to 5:

A score of __

1. The interaction manifested objectification, otherness, or righteousness.
2. The interaction manifested coldness and distance.
3. The interaction manifested indifference.
4. The interaction would be characterized as pleasant or cordial.
5. The interaction manifested love and gratitude.

There is a suggested ongoing practice for mapping and expanding your **Love Footprint™** presented in the companion course. Scan the QR code at the end of the chapter to access it.

I offer that every time you apply this scale honestly to the interactions you are having with others, you will awaken a new consciousness in yourself, a love consciousness.

It is powerful for each of us to pay attention to our individual **Love Footprint**, and devote our energy to a newly emerging and growing commitment to love on the planet. And as you work on this within yourself and your life, know that Sai Maa is at the same time actively anchoring a dimension of love on the planet.

What is meant by a "Dimension of Love" on the planet?

Think of two people loving each other. That exists, doesn't it? Now imagine the environment around them. Do they live in an environment of love?

Think about the air around you. What if there was smoke in the air around you? It would make a difference to you immediately, wouldn't it? What if—as real as what is physically around us—there is energy all around us? Literally an environment that we are living in that we have not been very conscious of.

What if that environment, like the air that we breathe, was filled with energy of fear, resentment, judgment, and opinions? Now, what if all of that was out of the environment and that environment was love energy, and nothing else? And what if that environment surrounded the whole planet, all the time?! Indeed, what if there existed a dimension of love for us to live inside of?

What if a dimension of love coming into existence for the planet depends upon what you and I are emanating all the time?!

Please keep reading. Together we can alter the **Love Footprint** of not only ourselves as individuals but also collectively as a society. Together we could anchor a dimension of love for the planet!

Fellow travelers we are indeed!

Your Love
Does Matter

Deepen your Work here.

SCAN
CODE

www.YourLoveDoesMatter.com

Chapter 5

TRANSFORMATIONAL
DISCOVERIES

This is the work of Transformation, bringing forth a
breakthrough in the possibility of being human.
　　　　　　　　　　　　　　　　　—Werner Erhard

Transformation happens when *anything* and *everything* becomes possible for us as human beings.

In the moment of transformation, we know ourselves as the authors of our own lives and know we are standing in front of a blank canvas—totally free and totally powerful to create ourselves and our living, from nothing. We are informed by the past yet not bound by it. All limiting beliefs have fallen away. We are called by the possibility of being fully alive and fully SELF-expressed. The moment of transformation is exhilarating.

I have led and witnessed firsthand the transformation of hundreds of thousands of people in many countries around the world. Being there for anyone's transformation is a breathtaking and humbling experience, as God within is ultimately unconcealed.

The results that we produce in the wake of transformation can be startling and outside of anything imaginable.

Over and over again, I have witnessed marriages that were in the hands of divorce lawyers be wholly and healthfully resurrected. Over and over again, I have watched children and parents, brothers and sisters who have not spoken for decades find one another and bestow grace upon one another. Over and over again, I have seen health issues disappear. Over and over again, I have witnessed important personal and professional projects that were never getting done, be completed with impressive excellence and startling velocity.

I assert that you and I can be truly free (e.g., free from resentments, judgments, regrets, hauntings from the past).

When We Are Free, We Love

I assert that when you and I are truly free, we love, naturally.

And I assert that the following three particularly transformational discoveries are essential for this freedom to be ourselves.

Again, I acknowledge the genius of Werner Erhard's ideas and programs, which allowed for these transformational discoveries I am sharing with you. I share these discoveries here with the permission of Landmark Worldwide, which owns the rights to and offers these programs. I invite you to discover them for yourself in your reading; if you would like to participate further with these inquiries, you could consider participating in the programs offered by Landmark www.landmarkworldwide.com.

Three Domains of Life: Be, Do, Have

You could say there are three domains of life:

- What we *have*
- What we *do*
- Who we *are* as human beings

What we *have* is simple ... we have cars, houses, clothes, moods, brothers and sisters, and so on.

What we *do* is simple ... we do dishes, we go to bed, we drive the car.

Who we *are* is less clear.

Consider there are ways of *being* ... kind/cruel, tender/cold, respectful/disrespectful, among others.

At every moment of our lives, (a) we have something(s), (b) there is/are something(s) we are doing; and (c) there is also some way we are *being*.

Can you notice that nobody ever talks to you about who you are *being*?! When was the last time you walked into a party and someone said, "Hi, who are you being?"

I am sure the answer is NEVER!

You walk into a party and people will discuss what you (a) have ("Hey where did you get that sweater?" or "Hi, do you have a boyfriend?").

They will often discuss what you are (b) doing ("Hi, are you taking that job?" or "Hi, are you going on vacation?").

But never (c), who are you being?

Why is that?

Consider that people talk about what they think matters for happiness, and *everyone* believes that what matters for your happiness is what you *have* and what you *do*! Consequently, that is what everyone talks about: What you have and what you do!

Also, what we have and what we do is obvious to the eye. You can see if I have a sweater. You can easily see if I am dancing. But who am I being? That is less obvious to the eye, isn't it?

Yes, most people (and you should probably consider you belong to the group "most people") live as though the quality of their life is given by (a) what they have and (b) what they do. The evidence for that is how much attention people pay to what they have and what they do, while paying virtually no attention to "Who they are Being."

My Beloved, pause for a moment and reflect on what you have been concerned about so far just today! Haven't your primary concerns been about what to *do* and what to *have*? And have you ever wondered about *who you are being*? And that is just today. What about the last 20 years? What have you been concerned about for the last 20 years?

Since *all* attention is paid to the false gods of DOING and HAVING, we *must* think the quality of our lives comes from those two domains: DOING and HAVING.

First, is that true for you? Investigate this assertion. What have you been talking about ... to yourself and others? Doing? Having? Haven't you been talking about what you and others have done and had, should do and have, ought to do and have, hope to do and have?

Think about it. Question it.

Virtually no one has discovered the utter fallacy of this view of life. Can you, now?

Start by questioning whether the quality of your life, your fundamental happiness, is really connected to those domains at all.

Pause reading for a moment and observe your own hand. Move your hand back and forth and observe the front of your hand moving with the back of your hand.

If the front moves, does the back move? Immediately? Always? Perfectly?

The relationship the front and back of your hands have is an amazing relationship to have. THEY GO EVERYWHERE TOGETHER, IMMEDIATELY AND EXACTLY.

Now reflect for a moment. Does your happiness and anything you *have* move together like that!?

Could you have a new car and be happy? A moment later could you have that same new car and be miserable? Could you have a romantic partner and be happy? A moment later could you have that same romantic partner and be sad? Yes! Discover for yourself that your happiness and anything you *have* are not connected at all! Maybe they just cross paths accidentally and occasionally.

What about what you are doing?

Could you be skiing in the Swiss Alps and be miserable? Could you be cleaning the house and be happy?

Yes! Discover for yourself that your happiness and anything you *do* are not connected at all! Certainly not like the front of your hand and the back of your hand!

Now examine the domain of Being. There are **ways of being**. Human beings are sometimes being generous and other times being stingy ... sometimes being forgiving and other times being resentful, sometimes being tender and other times being cold.

Discover for yourself that your happiness and your way of being do in fact move together like the front of your hand and the back of your hand: *always*, *immediately*, and *exactly*.

Moment by moment, if you love who you are being, you love your life. If you hate who you are, at the same moment you will be hating life. And it can all change in an instant!

Notice, you love being kind, and when you are being kind you are happy. Notice, you hate being stingy, and when you are being stingy you are not happy at all.

If you are friendly one moment and rude the next, your happiness will disappear in the same moment. Get friendly again and be happy again in the same exact moment!

TEST THIS OUT FOR YOURSELF.

This is GOOD NEWS!

Do we have any say about what we *have*? Could we have a car one moment and it's gone the next? Yes! Could we have a boyfriend one moment and he is gone the next? Yes! (Scoundrel!)

So if you believe your happiness is dependent upon anything you *have*, then you will be anxious in life as you deal with the fact that you actually have no say about what you *have*!

Do you have any say about what you do? If you step off a roof, will you go down?

Do you ultimately have a say about whether you breathe or not? No. So if you believe your happiness is dependent upon anything you *do*, then you will be anxious in life as you deal with your having no say about what you do!

Now, do you have a say about who you *are*?

Whether you are generous or stingy ... who is that up to?

Whether you are forgiving or resentful ... who is that up to?

Discover for yourself that your way of being may be the *one thing in life* you have *total say* about!

And if your happiness is connected perfectly and exactly to your way of being, then welcome the good news that you have total say about your own happiness!

What about the way another person treats you?

Discover for yourself that the way another treats you is something you *have* (e.g., you *have* someone in your life who is critical, rude, or cold. Or you *have* someone in your life who is caring and kind.)

Discover for yourself that if someone is being kind to you and you are rude, you are not happy. And vice versa. If someone is being rude to you and you are kind, your happiness is alive.

The way another person treats us has nothing to do with our happiness! Really!

Test it out. Please don't simply take my word for it.

The question then is, "What is the point of other people?" No one can give you anything—they can love you, but that does not have you experience love. Someone can be patient with you, but that does not have you experience patience. The only thing that has you experience love or patience, for example, is **YOU BEING LOVING** or **PATIENT!**

So, with that profound insight, do you wonder what the role of others is in your life?

Maybe the *only* thing others really provide us is the opportunity to *be*. Can you be tender if there is no one there to be tender with? Can you be respectful if there is no one there to respect? Can you be empowering if there is no one there to empower? Or does it require the presence of another for you to love who you are being and, therefore, love being you? When you get that, you may fall to your knees with gratitude ... gratitude for the really difficult people, for the very existence of that other person and their presence in your life. Imagine living being moved with gratitude for the presence of others in your life.

What about someone really difficult? Notice further that the more difficult another person is, the more it provides one thing and one thing only for you: the opportunity to be more of the person you love being! A polite clerk in a store allows you to be polite back. A rude clerk allows you to be really generous. A great boss allows you to be great. A difficult boss allows you to be a giant. A connected brother allows you to be connected. A distant brother allows you to be truly magnanimous. Yes, the more difficult another is, the bigger the opportunity for us. My Beloved, please check this out for yourself. Try it out. See what living from this point of view provides you!

*   *   *

Now my Beloved, let's examine LOVE as a way of being.

Most people relate to love as an emotion and say, "I feel love." Or people relate to Love as a thought process, "I think I am in Love."

What if feelings and thoughts are things you *have* (i.e., I have thoughts and I have feelings)?

And we have just established that what you *have* has nothing to do with your happiness or quality of life! You *have* emotions and you *have* thoughts. Does what you have impact your happiness? Not at all!

Or, likewise, people relate to love as something to do (e.g., send flowers).

But please examine this. Please see for yourself that sending flowers does not have Love to be there as a presence—you can send flowers while feeling resentful and thinking you are foolish. Love is not present, palpable, able to be experienced, is it?

That is right, my Beloveds. We are only interested in the *presence* of Love. We are not settling for the concept of Love. You can "know" you love somebody and even say something in the order of, "Of course I love her; she is my mother!" and yet there is absolutely no presence of love … nothing there palpable, able to be experienced.

Love is there as a presence only when we are *being* loving. In this case we would say, "I AM one who loves!" or "Love is who I AM!"

Now, while most people think life moves in the direction of

have
then *do*
then *be* …

> If we have loving feelings …
> and we take loving actions …
> then we will be Lovers.

Please catch yourself living inside that view of life:
If I have the right job …
and I do it the right way,
I will be successful.

Or:

If I have the right amount of money,
and I invest it the right way,
then I will be wealthy.

As we found out a few paragraphs ago, the problem with the above is how little say we have about what we have and what we do! Therefore, we find out we have based our happiness on something we have no say about.

Good News: Actually, life works in the reverse order ... be *then* do *then* have.

If I *am* forgiving,
and I take forgiving actions,
I will have a life filled with forgiveness.

If I *am* tender,
and I take tender actions,
I will have a life filled with tenderness.

What if we relate to Love as a way of being ... I am being Loving at any given moment.

Be, do, have is the actual direction of life in which life works!

My Beloved, are you Love? Then take Loving actions. Then have the life that Love would have!

*　　*　　*

Other Transformational Discoveries

It All Arises in Language

It is time to ask yourself, "What do I take for granted about the world that in fact may not be true at all?"

For instance, that the world is made up of objects and each object is separate and distinct from every other object. Do you take that for granted? Is it true?

Pause and look at the room around you. How does it appear to you?

Is there a table? Is that table separate and distinct from the chair? Are both the chair and the table separate and distinct from the lamp, and then from the rug, the book, the computer? Why do you see it that way? Is it really that way?

Do these seem like ridiculous questions? Think with me now. This journey we are on takes real thinking and thinking things we have never thought before and thinking things no one else ever said to us before.

Again, we see the world this way: The world is made up of objects and every object is separate and distinct from every other object.

Why do we see it that way?

Follow these steps of discovery:

Wonder (note: wonder is a very high state of consciousness rarely engaged in by most people) how anything becomes separate from anything else in our worldview.

How did the United States become separate from Canada? (Stop and notice that you do see the world that way ... that Canada is really separate from the U.S.). After all, there is just one piece of land, is there not? Consider that how Canada became separate from the U.S. is that *one* piece of land was given *two* names. Some of the land was named Canada and some of the land was named the United States, and in that instant one piece of land became two things, not one.

What about Monday and Tuesday? How did Monday become separate from Tuesday? Isn't it actually one block of time given two different names?

Now look at your own arm. One arm. Now add the name *hand* and notice that immediately one thing (your arm) is now two separate things: your arm and your hand! And you see it that way now, with your own eyes!

Yes, yes, yes, my Beloved. Try it again. Observe the room you are in. One room, correct? Now add names, for example *wall* and *window*. What happens to the one room? Yes, notice that with every name added it becomes two, then three, then four separate things.

Can you at least wonder: Is everything in fact separate from everything else? Or do we see it that way because of the names given? Were things separate and we named them, or was there only one universe and we separated the universe into billions of parts, in our own view, by doling out names?

When you were an infant, before you acquired language, was Monday separate from Tuesday, or were Monday and Tuesday only separated by the language you were taught?

Do boundaries exist in the universe or do boundaries only come into existence by virtue of *naming*? This is the oven, this is the sink—two things, except it actually is all one thing: the kitchen!

Test it. Look at the oven—one thing, correct? Look at the sink. Another, second thing, correct? You literally see two things. Now step back and look at the *kitchen* and notice that it all becomes *one* for you!

When you were an infant, did you see one toy as yours and another toy as theirs? Or you only see it that way *after* you were taught the word "mine!"?

Can you now ask yourself, "What comes first? Language or what I see?"

Ask yourself, "Am I really separate from my brother, or is it possible that we are we one being with two names, like arm and hand, Monday and Tuesday, wall and window?

Ask yourself, "Can one thing have different molecular structures?"

Does my body have blood and teeth and muscle? Different molecular structures and all one body, correct?

So now examine a table or desk. Do you see an end to the table and a beginning of the air? You do, don't you?!

But does the table really end there, or do the molecules simply disperse and thin out—and come together again in the area we call the wall?

So are you really separate from the air around you, or do you only see it that way because you were taught the words *you* and *air*, and in that moment, you were separated from the air forever?

When did you first see yourself as separate from your parents (and everyone else!)? Perhaps it was when one of your parents took their finger and pointed and said "Mommy" then "Daddy" then your name. They repeated that exercise over and over until one day you pointed your finger toward what they had named "Mommy," and you said "Mommy," and there was great celebration in the village!

They went further. A while later, someone came to you and said, "What is your name, Little Boy?" or "What is your name, Little Girl?"

And in my case, when I exclaimed "David," again the villagers were beside themselves with happiness—failing to notice I had just separated myself from the rest of humanity and God forever! I was now and only the singular thing called "David" and nothing and no one else!

Yes, my Beloveds … that is the power of language and the exact power of naming.

Is it useful? Yes. It is useful to call this house "your" house and that house "my" house. It is useful to call some time period Monday and some time period Tuesday. It is useful to call some humanity Bob and other humanity George. It lets us organize and work in the world a certain way. But is it true? Useful and true are not the same thing!

A Third Essential Transformational Discovery

Where Do Good and Bad, Right and Wrong, Should and Shouldn't Exist?

Take a moment and reflect on the fact that when we are several months old, we acquire the capacity for language.

How do we learn language? You're correct if you said we listen to the people around us who are already talking.

As you listened, what was everybody (without exception) always (without exception) saying?

Now, the topic of conversation varied. They could have been talking about

... the weather
... the price of gas
... what time your dad came home from work
... the firmness of the pasta
... capital punishment
... something the Pope said
... your handwriting
... how the bed was made
... the war
... the color of the hair of the lady next door
... your grandmother's cooking
... a TV show, movie, or book
... the legalization of marijuana
... the Holocaust
... your table manners

But no matter the topic, wasn't the context always the same? Weren't they always saying:

... that something was good—or it was bad (e.g., your handwriting)?
... that something was right—or it was wrong (e.g., a Supreme Court decision)?
... that something should have been—or shouldn't have been the way it was (e.g., the length of the grass in the front yard)?

And while that context goes unnoticed, it is constantly applied to every detail of life and existence.

But please, dear reader, stop and take nothing for granted. There is more to discover here!

Yes, the whole world (including you and me) has been taught the words *right/wrong, good/bad, should/shouldn't*.

And now we literally see everything through those filters!

Please confirm this for yourself.

When you wake up, do you see weather, or do you automatically see good weather or bad weather?

When you watch a movie, don't you automatically relate to it as a good movie or a bad movie?

When you are in traffic, isn't it good traffic or bad traffic?

When someone tells you their political view of who the best candidate is, aren't they right or wrong?

When you learn how much someone tipped the server, didn't they tip as much as they should have or shouldn't have?

When you are waiting in the doctor's office, isn't there a length of time you should have to wait or shouldn't have to wait?

Now I ask again, my Beloved, do good/bad, right/ wrong, should/shouldn't really exist?

We see it and hear it all everywhere, don't we?

So it *must* be there. But where is it?

Let's pause for a moment and look carefully.

Do we see the world first, *or* do we learn words first and then see only and always exactly what that word we learned describes?

Test this out for yourself.

Were you taught the words *near* and *far*? Is anything *really* near or far?

Is the closest grocery store near or far?

What if you had no car, then what would you say?

What if you had exactly 10 minutes to get there, then what would you say?

So now can we ask, is the store near or far? Or is the store only *exactly where it is* and whether it is near or far exists *only* in our *speaking about* the store?

Were you taught the words *tall* and *short*?

Now as you look at people do you see tall people and short people? I bet you do.

But are they tall or short? Or are they only and exactly the height they are?

Were you taught words that have you see things a certain way (e.g., as tall or short) when those qualities do not exist in the thing itself?

If someone is 6 feet in height, do you see them as tall? Now go examine them closely. Can you find any "tall" where they are? Or do you see them as tall only after you were taught the word tall?

We learn words and then we see the world through the words we learned.

Why do medical students spend the first period of study learning terms? Would they be able to see what they need to see if they had not learned the terms?

Did you ever learn the term *corpus callosum*? If you have learned the term *corpus callosum*, then when I show you a human brain you will see it, but if you never learned the term *corpus callosum*, if I show you a human brain you will just see the brain as a whole and not see or recognize the corpus callosum!

If you were never taught the word *onomatopoeia*, then you would never hear it!

 It is important to discover for yourself that *language has us see things that are not there*! If I ask you to describe this image, I could ask, "what direction is it?" and you will say "*up!*" If I ask, "what number is it?" you will say "*one!*" If I ask, "what body part is it?" you will say "*finger!*" But is there any "*up*" there? Is there any "*one*" there? Is there any "*finger*" there?

We see what the language we are given has us see.

You can see "bad" in a child hitting another child. But is there any bad *there*, or is there only and exactly a child hitting another child?

Where does the bad exist? That is correct … *only and exactly in our language about* the child hitting another child.

So here is a shocking revelation about the world: Good and bad, right and wrong exist *only in our speaking about* the world and not at all in the world itself.

I have good news for you: You will never be a bad person because bad does not exist. Someone may say you are bad, but that is decisively different than you actually being bad.

I have bad news for you: You will never be a good person either— because there is no such thing! There are only people we say are good and bad, and no one is good or bad!

If this is the case, then when you speak, do you engender a view of the world? If I say my boss is a jerk, do I then engender anyone listening to see "jerkdom" where my boss is?

If I say my dad is closed-minded, do I engender anyone listening to start seeing evidence of his being closed-minded? Really, how does the way he combs his hair become evidence that he is closed-minded? Oh. Because we called him closed-minded and now we see it!

Yes … speaking *precedes* seeing!

So every time you speak, do you create reality for whoever listens?

Could I say my brother is unforgivable?

If I do, what happens for anyone who listens to me say that?

If I say my brother deserves honor, what happens for anyone who listens to me say that?

Is one of those statements more difficult than the other to say?

Here is a trick question: Which of those statements is true?

The answer is *neither*! They are both possible views expressed now in language.

There is a difference between truth and reality.

Here is a difficult lesson. What have you said? What did your speaking have you and others see?

Do you now have things you have said you wish you hadn't said?

Do you now have things you have not said you wish you had said?

Imagine you are a parent and you know that one of your child's current teachers said to your child's future teacher, "This child is a problem and will be nothing but trouble for you!"

What is the effect of listening to that on the future teacher? What does the future teacher start seeing and hearing when they are with your child?

Doesn't this break your heart?

What would you like to say now, with the recognition that whoever listens to you will start seeing what you speak into existence?

What would you like to say about your parents, your spouse, your children, your coworkers, your president, people of a certain race, people of a certain religion, people with disabilities? What do you want to say, knowing that whoever listens to you will start seeing in that person/those people what you just spoke into existence?

How thoughtful could you be about what you say? How purposeful could you be about what you're about to say, knowing that what you say creates a reality for whoever listens to you?

(Join me in the companion course for a talk I did on this topic. Scan the QR code at the beginning or end of the book.)

Chapter 6

A FULL AWAKENING

*Our heart knows what our mind has forgotten—it knows
the sacred that is within all that exists, and through
a depth of feeling we can once again experience this
connection, this belonging.*
—Llewellyn Vaughan-Lee

I had those "transformational discoveries" between 1983 and 2000.

Now I would like to share with you what would be considered a "spiritual awakening" that opened other unexpected new doors to a world I didn't even know existed.

In 2010, I walked into a large hotel ballroom in Vail, Colorado, where well over a thousand people were gathered for an event with Her Holiness Jagadguru Sai Maa.

On that first day, meeting Sai Maa for the very first time, Sai Maa called me up on the platform and invited me to put my head on her lap, and then she tenderly brushed my back—my first experience of being loved by the Divine—my first experience of love from the other side of the veil!

There are no words that do justice to this experience. "ETER-NAL TRUTH" may come close. God's Love, God's Grace infused every cell of my body, every dimension of my being. There was everything (e.g., joy, abundance, light, gratitude, perfection, clarity, bliss, all time, every-where-ness) and there was nothing (i.e., timelessness, formlessness, silence, no-where-ness, neither darkness nor light but ultimate transparency, stillness—physical, mental, spiritual).

I knew (as in knowing versus thinking, hoping, aspiring) that I am loved by God. In that moment, I experienced perfection in being human.

The experience was undebatable, unforgettable, and undeniable. After some time of gently brushing my back, Sai Maa leaned forward and whispered in my ear, "That is complete now. I have been brushing away your karma; it is gone now. You are free."

And so it is.

Now you might understand why it is that when Sai Maa comes into my presence I will fall to my knees with reverent gratitude.

Now you might understand why it is that when I was given the chance to bathe Sai Maa's feet in sacred water, I wept with joy.

Discovering what had always been true, is true now, will always be true. It is eternally true that there is an ever-present, everywhere energy of Creator, Source, God, Divinity—that if we open ourselves to experience this, it feels like being wrapped in and imbued with euphoric, tender Love.

Dear Reader, pause now and be aware of what surrounds you. Can you feel an energy touching the skin of your face? That is it. Now can you feel it touching the crown of your head? Yes, that is it! Now can you feel it pulsating softly in the cells of your blood, the cells of your body? Yes, that is it too!

Now, most importantly, at this moment, give back the belief that there is a "you" separate from everything else to the teachers who convinced you of that. Be willing to call all of "that"—that energy of Grace, that life force of God (i.e., Prana)—be willing to call it "Me!" Try saying it out loud: "This is Me!" "I am this love, I am this energy of life, I am this energy of God." Go further and say: "I am this love that is everywhere, all at once, all the time—yes, this is me!"

My Beloved, begin to wonder what is possible for you, for us, with this awakening!

My 23-year-old twin grandchildren live in Connecticut, about a five-hour drive from my house. If I had my way, I would be with them physically every day. I would hug them and kiss them every day and tell them they are perfect, beautiful, and loved. Imagine the joy I now have knowing that in the absence of that five-hour drive, I am already and always where they are, surrounding them as Love, as light, as Grace.

Try this now: Bring someone you are committed to love into your awareness; someone who is not with you physically. Now, be aware of the energy that surrounds this person and make real for yourself: "There I am, This is me!" Now activate the love of that energy so that it wraps them, as if in a soft, beautiful blanket.

Yes, there you are, with them, loving them! Is it any less real than if they were physically in your presence? Keep experimenting with this until there is no difference for you between expressing your love with them physically present and expressing your love no matter where you and they are physically.

By the way, there is science to this! If you are interested in current research and applications, you could check out the research of "HeartMath" (https://www.heartmath.org/).

*   *   *

The term *Jagadguru* means "Guru for the world," and it is an official designation.

Global enlightenment is Sai Maa's mission.

With infinite compassion, Her Holiness Sai Maa also sets an example as an international humanitarian leader. Wherever she goes, she uplifts and supports those around her, creating pathways to relieve the pain and suffering of humanity, in numbers great and small:

- Giving abused and disadvantaged women the economic and educational tools they need to reclaim their lives with dignity
- Stepping in to restore normalcy to those who have lost their home to floods, hurricanes, and earthquakes
- Preventing blindness and performing cataract operations in India, where vision problems are common
- Helping meet the basic needs of children who are suffering around the world
- Providing food in India, home to the largest undernourished population in the world

Chapter 7

I Am That I Am

*Man will realize his mission on earth when he knows
himself as divine and reveres others as divine.*
—Sathya Sai Baba

This book, Your *Love* Does *Matter*, is needed and wanted now at this point in our evolution as a civilization.

What is needed and wanted now for humanity requires a fundamentally new identification of Self, who we consider ourselves to be, who we think of ourselves as, said most rigorously: who we are, that we are? Said another way, what is needed and wanted next for humanity is a new finish to the declaration: "I am that I am _____."

Why is the question phrased as "Who are you, that you are?" instead of "Who are you?" The answer is because it happens that a person *is* something but has absolutely no relationship to that which they *are*. For example, a person could actually be a father (biologically). He is a father, as a matter of fact, and knows it. And yet, that same person may *not* relate to himself as a father at all. He might have zero thoughts, zero emotions, and take zero actions related to being a father. On the other hand, a father that is—that *he is* a father—will without question have the thoughts and emotions and take the actions consistent with being a father.

Today, anyone who is asked, "Who are you, that you are?" has an answer, whether they are aware of having that answer or not.

In other words, if I asked you, "Who are you?" you might reply with "I am not sure." You might be unaware that there is a definite *you that you are* and equally unaware that your thoughts, emotions, and actions are shaped by that reality.

For you, your answer to the question "Who are you that you are?" does not live like an answer to that question; it lives simply as the way life is ... the truth about life.

Fundamental to everyone's answer is:

I am that I am my body.

> Don't we have thoughts related to being our body? If I ask you to point to yourself, do you not point to your body?

> Don't we have emotions that indicate we relate to our bodies as who we are?

> For those of us who are overweight, do we not feel embarrassed or ashamed?

> Don't we take actions related to being our bodies? When we say "I" am tired, don't we go lay down our body?

I am that I am my thoughts.

> Don't we say, "I think this and I think that"?

Don't we get upset if someone disagrees with us, and don't we defend our thoughts like we are defending ourselves?

I am that I am my emotions.

Don't you relate to someone not attending to your feelings as if they are insulting YOU?

I am that I am my history.

Don't we say, "I did this" or "This happened to me"?

Don't we feel pride about some things we have done and embarrassment about others?

Don't we present our resumes as a way of introducing our "selves" to prospective employers?

I am that I am this and not that

Don't we say, "I am wearing a jacket," signaling that the jacket is on us but is not us?

Don't we feed ourselves and not others?

Don't we let our cars be dirty, while we take daily showers?

My Beloved, think this through now for yourself.

I am that I am an object existing in a universe of objects, and I am that I am separate from every other object in the universe.

I am that I am in a world where everything is right or wrong, good or bad, and should or shouldn't be the way it is.

Now, dear reader, investigate this for yourself. Please do not just read this. Sit for a few minutes and ask yourself, or with someone else, and explore the question, "I am that I am (who/what)?" Said less rigorously, "What is real for me is that I am _____ or I think of myself as _____."

What is your answer? Isn't your answer a version of:

I am that I am my body (i.e., if I ask you to point to yourself, do you not point in the direction of the body?)

I am that I am my thoughts (said another way: I am the one that thinks what I think)

I am that I am my emotions (said another way: I am the one that feels what I feel)

I am that I am my history (said another way: I am the one who has gone through what I have gone through and done what I have done)

I am that I am this and I am not that (e.g., I am this body and not the air around it)

I am that I am one object existing in a universe of objects, and I am that I am separate from every other object in the universe

I am that I am in a world where everything is right or wrong, good or bad, and should or shouldn't be the way it is.

[Join me in the companion course for a talk I did on this topic. Scan the QR code at the beginning of the book.]

As a consequence, what do you defend when you defend your "Self"?

Isn't a **new consciousness** required for the next step in our evolution?

Won't we take a giant step in our evolution when we can authentically say:

I am that I am eternal light,
I am that I am eternal love,
I am that I am everywhere, all at once, all the time,
I am that I am creator, and I am that I am all that is created?

Won't we take a giant step in our evolution when as a society we are responsible for our **Love Footprint**?

And won't we take a giant step in our evolution when we confront that the whole *paradigm* of right/wrong, good/bad, and should/shouldn't is:

a) completely fabricated
b) not at all effective
c) detrimental to all human relationships and individual self-love.

When we literally take that *paradigm* **out of existence** and replace it with a paradigm simply of *what works and does not work,* then and only then will we be truly free to love.

Can we explore all of this together in this book?

Chapter 8

NEW EXPRESSIONS

For it was not into my ear that you whispered but into my heart.
It was not my lips you kissed but my soul.
                                                —Judy Garland

I have recently performed wedding ceremonies, memorial services, and Sunday sermons. I have included one of each here. In each, the participants were called to go within and own their love, experience their love, and share their love … right there on the spot.

Dear reader, imagine being in the audience of these events and imagine that these services were written for you. Participate in them as you read them. A new possibility of love between us as humans is offered. Step into it, my Beloved.

Please enjoy this wedding. Can you hear a new foundation for any marriage?

Jo and Ryan's Wedding, September 16, 2023

Cindy and Henry, do you invite Ryan into your family and bless this marriage?

On behalf of Jo and Ryan: welcome, everyone, to Big Skye Ranch.

Each of us is here to celebrate and bestow grace upon this union of Ryan and Jo.

It is in the presence of us, this community of loving family and friends, that Jo and Ryan will commit to each other.

It is in the embrace of this community that this couple will be cared for.

And for decades to come, it is in the commitment and intention of this community that Jo and Ryan will thrive.

Indeed, it is in the blessing of this community that Jo and Ryan will live in a state of grace.

Create your witnessing this marriage as both a sacred privilege and sacred duty. It does matter that each of us is here, and it does matter that we are here together.

Let's take a moment and gather the power of our collective love.

As you look upon Jo and Ryan, lift your hand to your heart, as if you are bringing them and holding them in a most precious place, there, in your heart.

Now they have a home in all of our hearts.

Acknowledge yourself as one who loves deeply; tonight our love is especially for Jo and Ryan. And now let's extend that love to each other.

Turn to the people around you; some you may know, some may be strangers just happening to sit near you; it does not matter!

Now take a moment and express your love for each other, or wish each other peace with the simple statement, "may peace be with you"… or maybe say "thank you," or "thank you for being here this evening to bless this marriage."

Do that now …

Now look up for a moment at the big sky above us all.

Let yourself be struck by the awareness that every man, woman, and child on the planet is under this same sky.

And let's take a moment of quietness and wish all people well, wish all people peace, and wish all the people of this earth to know they are loved.

Thank you … it is this environment of our collective love for humanity that Jo and Ryan will be married.

Jo and Ryan, I now invite you to hold each other's hands. Look into each other's eyes … and discover each other newly here.

Now look into each other's eyes and see each other's strength.

Look into each other's eyes and see other's frailty.

Take a moment and see each other's courage.

And then see each other's uncertainty, an uncertainty that is calmed by being together.

And now look into each other's eyes and see each other's dreams.

See each other's dreams.

And enjoy that it is not Jo's dream or Ryan's dream … it is a dream you share.

It is your shared dream, which you will always be able to find in each other's eyes.

Now let yourself be grateful,

Grateful that from the moment you were born …

Every breath you have each taken;

Every step you have each taken;

Every joy and every heartbreak you have had,

Every triumph and every defeat you have ever experienced,

Every moment of the entire life you have lived

Has led you here, now.

To this perfect moment

To be together

To commit to each other

To marry each other

In the presence of this community that loves you more than words can express, yes, be filled with gratitude for each other, for this moment.

Now take a moment and look out at this community and let yourself be embraced by our prayers—embraced by our blessings and embraced by our love.

And it could go unsaid, but I want to say how deeply grateful I am that you invited me to perform this ceremony.

Let's proceed.

Let's create a powerful context for this marriage.

Being Versus Having

At the end of the day, whether we love our life or not is not given by what we have, not even given by what we do, but given entirely by who we "be" as human beings.

We can have all the riches in the world and go to all the seven wonders, but if while we are there, we are closed-hearted, or stingy, or blaming, or resentful, we will not experience joy.

And if we have no riches and we are sweeping the streets,

And yet our hearts are open, and we are generous and forgiving, then we will indeed be joyous to be alive.

When one says to another, "I take you as my beloved forever," and becomes our husband or becomes our wife, they give us a totally unique opportunity that no one else does ... they put their whole life in our hands.

And in that moment, we have the privilege of being someone who has another thrive, has another be loved, has another be empowered, has another's dreams be fulfilled for their whole life. That is the true joy of being alive.

It is a mistake to enter marriage thinking I am supposed to get something from the other, thinking I am supposed to get love or get respect.

If the other loves us while we are closed, our life is empty, no matter how much they are loving us.

If the other is honoring us while we are judging them, there is no joy in being with them.

If the other cares for us while we are being uncaring, then the joy of being together is lost.

So as you enter this new life as husband and wife, you are entering the world where being true to who you really are ... being caring, being creative, being responsible, generous, kind, empowering, honoring, loving, and indeed adoring of the other is where and only where your joy and fulfillment will be found.

Now, what actually establishes a relationship is the giving of and honoring of one's word to each other. The giving of and honoring of one's word to each other creates a foundation as solid as this ground we are standing on to live from, to guide you through any challenges, to guide the life you create together.

There is no relationship, there is no marriage ... then you speak, you give your word to each other, and the relationship that is created in that moment is your creation.

In recognition of the power you have to bring into existence from nothing, the miracle of being related ... the miracle of being related as a matter of your word ... you choose to give your word to the following:

You promise that whenever you speak of each other to others, whoever that may be—family, friends, strangers—Jo, you promise that after you speak, whoever is listening will only be left with a deep respect of Ryan. And Ryan, you promise that after you speak, whoever is listening will only be left with a deep respect for Jo.

To this, do you give your word?

You promise to love and honor each other's family.

You are each joining a family that existed long before you met, to bring only love, peace, and deep gratitude to that family.

To this, do you each give your word?

You promise to live in the understanding that your experience does not come from the other. It is only when you love that you will experience love.

It is only when you honor that you will experience honor.

It is only when you are tender that you will experience tenderness. To live in this understanding.

To this, do you give your word?

You promise to live together in a world of communication, openness, and love ...

To this, do you give your word?

Now, will you exchange rings to symbolize the eternity of your marriage? Ryan, in giving Jo this ring, do you take her as your beloved forever?

Jo, in giving Ryan this ring, do you take him as your beloved forever?

I invite you now to share a kiss and seal this declaration.

Everyone, I present to you for this first time as husband and wife: Ryan and Jo.

*　　*　　*

My Beloved Reader: What are you experiencing right now? Be awake to the love you are experiencing, the love that you are.

Isn't it wonderful (and possible) to bring forth love, anywhere, anytime?

*　　*　　*

Oliver's Memorial

My Beloveds, beautiful, sweet Oliver committed suicide at age 17, on May 31, 2022.

His family asked me to lead a memorial service at the Friends Meeting House in Philadelphia that was attended by nearly 500 people, including many of his school classmates. What follows is the text of the service. Imagine being there and let your heart be open to the profound, deep love that reverberates in grief.

*　　*　　*

Good Morning,

With deep gratitude, I thank you for gathering here to celebrate Oliver.

We have strived today to design a gathering that Oliver might design himself.

Let us begin:

> When a soldier dies, we must pick up their flag and carry it.
>
> When a leader dies, we must know their vision and carry it as ours.
>
> When a son dies, we must go to his parents and bestow grace.
>
> When a brother dies, we must go to his brother and understand nothing is simple, nothing is easily said, and he must know that there is no way we need him to be, nothing we need him to do; we are simply grateful to be with him.
>
> When a friend dies, we must embrace one another and go out of our way to make vivid our appreciation of, indeed our love for, one another.
>
> When a child dies, we must love his spirit as we loved his body and set his spirit free to fly with the angels.

Today, we are gathered for all of that. In this historic meeting house, where for hundreds of years people have gathered in the name of love, in the name of peace, in honor of that which moves the human spirit,

We are here

> ... To pick up Oliver's flag of kindness and his vision for humanity and carry it as our own
>
> ... To bestow grace on this family
>
> ... To embrace this brother

... To make vivid our love for one another, and to wish Oliver's spirit the most beautiful existence with the angels.

Oliver is known by people as bringing a bright spirit wherever he went.

From his younger days playing baseball to his love of professional soccer, to playing Ultimate Frisbee in high school ... he delighted in the strategy and camaraderie of a good game.

He is described by many as open, curious, and generous. He saw the world in 3D and brought his brilliance to conversations.

Oliver was unafraid to challenge the way people viewed things and was also open to expanding his views. His insight and humor contributed to the people around him.

Oliver attended St. Joe's Prep and valued the spirit and community of the school. Oliver also dealt with major health challenges for over 4 years, and he needed to leave his sophomore year to tend to his health. He was determined to return his junior year and worked hard to do so. He considered this to be a major accomplishment of which he was proud. In the latter part of his senior year, he took a medical leave of absence. While working through his health issues, he did the work to complete his senior year and graduate with his class. He looked forward to going to Kenyon, where he believed he found a community of people who were like-minded and where he would thrive.

Oliver was a passionate person, and this came through in many ways from the classroom activities he chose to engage in and support other people in. He jumped in and helped a friend during the beginning of Garden Club. He was active in Ultimate Frisbee, serving as a captain. He instituted the popular intramural frisbee league this past winter, resulting in the participation of over 100 students.

He was instrumental in helping the team be recognized as a varsity sport at the Prep.

In thoughtful notes, many fellow students and others have given insight into Oliver. Through their words, Oliver's kindness comes shining through.

The music you have listened to while gathering is one of Oliver's playlists.

Oliver had a particular connection to the song "Imagine" and enjoyed playing it on his keyboard. As you listen to this now, let the music transport you to a space of peace, a space where your heart remembers its love of all mankind.

Note to reader: I invite you to pause now and listen to a recording of the song "Imagine."

Your Love
Does Matter

JOHN LENNON IMAGINE

SCAN CODE

We believe Oliver would want this gathering to be poignant with each person experiencing being loved, celebrated, and having the experience of being perfect exactly the way you are.

Please take a moment with a few people around you, those you know and those you have never met, and let any awkwardness just be there, and take a few moments to connect with each other.

… seize the moment to express gratitude for each other being here and wish each other peace.

Offer each other any blessing it pleases you to offer.

And take time to look each other in the eye and recognize each other, without knowing maybe each other's history, recognizing each other as fellow human beings carrying a common dream of peace on earth and goodwill toward man.

… let your heart be filled with gratitude for this person, going through what they have and will go through in life, never giving up the dream for peace on earth.

A person's life lives after the body is gone, in what is said of the person by those who knew them and were lucky enough and awake enough to recognize the gift this person's living was to them.

Oliver embraced his intellect, which was important to him, and it was delightful to everybody else.

And now some of you may wish to share with the rest of us your love of Oliver.

We will open the microphone now for those of you that wish to share. Before, however, turn to the people around you and share anything you would like to share of your relationship with Oliver, and enjoy this opportunity to celebrate his existence and that your paths did cross however they did.

Another song Oliver was especially connected with was "Let It Be." As you listen to this music, you could imagine Oliver sending this message directly to you. Also feel free to sing along if it becomes irresistible.

To close today, I will give you a message from Oliver. In his final note he said, "Tell everyone that cared, I love them." That he says "I love them" in present tense and not past tense is no mistake.

So, for those of you that cared, Oliver loves you.

Thank you.

* * *

My Beloved Reader: What are you experiencing right now? Again, be awake to the love you are experiencing, the love that you are.

* * *

This is a sermon I delivered at a small Methodist church, one week when the regular pastor was on vacation.

What does it take to live a life of loving, and what stops us?

I invite you to think this through as you read this sermon.

A Sunday Sermon

My Beloveds, imagine sitting in this congregation and being provoked to think something you have never thought before, that is absolutely essential to loving in the example of Christ. I do pray that no matter what religion is important to you, that you can appreciate the example that Christ is, just as no matter what nationality you may honor, you can appreciate the example that Gandhi is.

Sunday, June 2023

Welcome.

It is my privilege to lead us in worship again this morning with Pastor Shirley on vacation.

Let's start with a prayer.

Dear Lord:

We praise God from whom all blessings flow.

We are filled with gratitude as we acknowledge these blessings.

We are grateful for being blessed with this church: a simple and plain church that has stood here for all these years so that we now, here today, have a place to come and worship.

We are grateful for being blessed with one another: that each of us comes and together we create a community of worship that strengthens each of us in our faith.

We are grateful for being blessed with Pastor Shirley, our pastor who leads us week after week in our celebration of the life of Christ and the possibility of our living in Christ's example.

We are grateful for being blessed with the breath of life and the opportunity we have to be of service to others.

Yes, we praise God from whom all blessings flow. Amen.

Now the choir will treat us with a prelude this morning.

As we listen, I invite you to hear this song as your prayer.

Whatever the choir sings expresses your faith.

We can have their voice send our message to God.

Prelude

The call to worship:

Me: How blessed are we that God is love!

All: For all those times when we have experienced God's grace.

Me: We are alive with God's love!

All: Now is the time to joyfully accept the newness of life that God constantly offers to us.

Me: Come, let us celebrate the infinite and eternal love of God.

All: Let us open our hearts to the peace and joy of God. Amen.

Hymn number 700. "Abide with Me."

Me: The peace of Christ be with you.

All: And also with you, amen.

Everyone … please take a moment to be present to the others here and wish them the peace of Christ.

Scripture today: First, Psalm 139 verse 3:

Thou compassest my path and my lying down and art acquainted with all my ways.

Then, 1st Samuel 16 verse 7: The Lord seeth not as man seeth for man looketh on the outward appearance, but the Lord looketh upon the heart.

And, finally, John 3 verses 16 and 17:

For God so loved the world that he gave his only begotten son that whosoever believeth in him should not perish but have everlasting life.

For God sent not his son into the world to condemn the world, but that the world through him might be saved.

Me: This is the word of God for the people of God.

All: Thanks be to God, amen.

First, we are told God is with us always.

Then we learn from Christ's example what it looks like to see God in others and relate to every single human being, with no exception, as a child of God.

Whether that be the leper, the blind man, the woman being stoned, or finally the Roman guards who put him on the cross. Where he said, as recorded in Luke 23 verse 34: Father, forgive them, for they know not what they do.

It is important there to realize forgiveness is uniquely distinguished:

1) Not as condoning what was done
2) Not as making what was done acceptable

Simply loving unconditionally, bestowing grace, giving love that does not have to be deserved and can never be taken away.

That was Christ's love for all people, the grace he bestowed on all.

Relating to each, even the Roman guards, as children of God.

Now as Christians we challenge ourselves to live in the example of Christ!

And yet we so often find ourselves judging others, resenting others, unable to have our hearts filled with love—indeed, to bestow grace on others.

Again, offering love that does not have to be deserved and is never, never taken away.

Why do we find loving that way so hard?

Consider it is simple. We are not free.

We are imprisoned by our opinions of others.

We are imprisoned by our judgment of others.

We are imprisoned by the thoughts we have about others; the gossip we hear about them.

We are imprisoned by our view of others.

We often find ourselves resenting or judging and therefore not able to enjoy or in fact fighting with those that matter the most to us: our own parents, our own brothers and sisters, our lovers, our neighbors, the people we work with.

It is important to find yourself in this prison … only people who know they are in prison want out.

It is important to recognize how trapped we are. None of us would say, "I want to resent this person, I want to judge this person,

I want to fight my brother, my sister, my spouse, my child." And yet we do ... trapped in a world of opinion, judgment, and resentment.

We are so trapped, we even have opinions about opinions. Just notice what you think about opinionated people!

Recognizing that we are trapped in opinions immediately opens up the possibility of being free.

Free to love, free to love as Christ loved ... just loving ... bestowing grace.

What gives us freedom from the opinions and judgments that trap us?

Simple, actually: It is acknowledging that opinions are a view of someone and not the truth about them.

We see them a certain way and then believe that they are the way we see them.

We fail to notice that we speak first ... and then we see what we speak.

I show you this [show two fingers here] and I say it is a number, and you see two.

I show you this and say it is a universal symbol, and you see a peace sign.

What is spoken comes before what is seen and determines what is seen.

I say my father is closed-minded and then I watch him read a magazine and see the evidence for my sentence of him that he is closed-minded when in reality he is reading a magazine. There is no closed-minded in my father.

If a surgeon cut him open, there would be no closed-mindedness found. There would be bones and muscles found.

If a surgeon cut open someone you see as stupid, the surgeon would find no stupidity.

If the surgeon cut open someone you are sure is wrong, the surgeon would find no wrongness.

And yet we are sure it is there ... we see it and have evidence for it.

Failing to notice we called them wrong or we called them bad or we even called them unforgivable and then, *and only then*, we immediately began to see them that way.

Christ did not. He called them children of God and saw children of God in them. He said everyone was worthy of love and forgiveness and then saw each and every one as that.

Why do we say what we say about people? Simple. When we were taught language, we were taught views. The views came with the language.

If we can, simply acknowledge that the wrong we see in another is not in them.

Then we can be out of the prison of our opinions and love as Christ loves.

A surgeon would not find "wrong" in them ... we see it only because we said it.

If we can simply recognize that nothing we say about another is true about them—it is our view of them—then we are out of the prison of our judgment and can love as Christ loved.

Two more points:

1) It is important to recognize that you don't make up your thoughts—they just happen. So when you have a thought such as "This person is wrong," you never chose to think it; the thought just happened. It is part of being human, it is automatic: You have no say about the thoughts you have; they just come and go.

2) Something that is spoken only stays in existence as long as it is spoken.

My dad is wrong ...
My dad deserves honor

So, you speak and then you see.

Practice that as you practice living in the example of Christ.

Practice saying, "I see the God in you," and then be surprised and delighted that you start seeing it.

Yes, it is simple and it is profound.

Speak first.

This one, this one I have been judging, this one I have been resenting, this one is a child of God. And then notice you see them differently. And when you see them differently, newly you can love them newly.

I would like to leave with you with a beautiful voice.

I am going to play a recording of a young ten-year-old boy named Christopher Duffley.

Blind, autistic, and singing.

Open the eyes of my heart, Lord

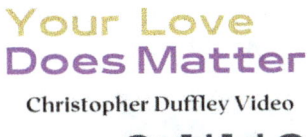

Christopher Duffley Video

Let us pray.

Lord, may we see with the eyes of our heart.

May our hearts be filled with Christ's love for all people.

May we bring a new dimension of love to this world. Seeing God in others and loving as Christ loves.

Amen.

I leave you with this simple benediction:

May you see with the eyes of your heart and be filled with the joy of loving.

Chapter 9

DEVOTION

Not to confuse devotion and emotions. Emotions change
all the time. Devotion is authentic, is real.
—Her Holiness Jagadguru Sai Maa

Sai Maa brought Mary Magdalene to my awareness.
In discovering the energy of Mary Magdalene, I was overcome,
being called to devotion. Mary's devotion to Master Jesus is breathtaking in its purity.

Painting of Mary Magdalena by Britten, www.studiobritten.com

Devotion answers all yearnings.

The question is: To whom or what would you be devoted?

For 35 years, I worked 18-hour days and was away from home as many as 300 days a year. What made all that worth it? What was I devoted to?

The program I led for those 35 years was called the Landmark Forum. The program was always Friday, Saturday, Sunday, and Tuesday evenings, except in Israel where the schedule was altered to allow for the Sabbath being honored.

On Sunday afternoon of that program, each participant was set totally free from any suffering, regrets, or resentments, any limiting beliefs, and totally free from their past. On Sunday afternoon, their *entire* slate was clean, and they have a future with nothing in it (which is the only true freedom … a future with nothing in it where anything and everything is possible). It was a sacred experience for every single program. Another way to express it (my words, not Landmark's words) was that each person experienced the God force (prana) within … experienced themselves as creator and creation, *and* whatever they created was so pure because it was being created from nothing. Whatever they created as a possibility for themselves and their life was pure possibility—no agenda, no should, no right, no wrong—simply a pure expression of creation. It always sounds like the words of God, because it comes from that energy. It is always an expression of love in its purest form. And each person in that moment was always moved to the depths of their soul by themselves and the possibility of creation itself. Again, the Sanskrit word for this is *prana*.

In hindsight, I realize I was devoted to this expression of the energy of prana. My love for each person, my love for their freedom, my love for the God within each being, felt in their hearts and expressed in their words and actions … to that I am devoted.

I sent the following to Maa while Maa was in Japan:

Bliss is in Devotion
Devotion to my Guru
Devotion to my Queen
Devotion to Source
Devotion to all that Maa is
I pranam at the feet of my greatest love

Maa replied instantly:

O My Sweetheart
You must be receiving what is happening here.
Devotion
Devotion
Devotion
Eternally …

Again, devotion is maybe the highest love. The question is what am I devoted to? Sai Maa the person? Yes, I love Maa so much that I have often welled up with tears at the thought of it.

But that is not it, really. Is it Sai Maa's teachings that I am devoted to? Yes, but more than that.

It is the prana, the life force, life breath, God energy that flows through the body, the chakras; that pulsates in every cell and every strand of DNA.

Prana is not human. Prana does not have a human form or a human face. And yet prana lives and loves. Prana bestows grace on every molecule of creation. All is perfect in the "eyes" of prana. Prana is heaven on earth. Prana is "Thy will be done." Prana is "on earth as it is in heaven."

I am devoted to prana. I beg for prana to be everywhere, with everyone and everything. I beg for prana to be loving all, indeed blessing all with its tender kiss and embrace.

When we love, prana fills our hearts and minds. Yes, my Beloved, you are infused with prana. That is your beauty. That is the source of any and all serenity you experience. Prana in every breath.

Pause. Be quiet. Breathe. Be aware ... what gives the breathing, be aware, what is in the breath? Is there energy in the breath? Is there life in the breath? Do you have to do something for that life to be there, or is it there as a miraculous gift? Be still. Breathe. Notice. What is in the breath? Of course there is what we call air. But observe more keenly. When you breathe, do you live?

Yes, yes, it is the source of life. Does your breath love you? Yes, yes. It is there for you ... never judging, never scolding ... simply giving you life. That is love. The love of prana for you. That is Grace. Love you never have to deserve, simply given to you.

Now my Beloveds, every time you inhale you fill your lungs ... your chest expands, your heart has room to love.

To you, my beloved reader:

To the prana that is in each of your cells and your DNA itself—to God as a presence in your heart and in your words and actions, to your creation of love as a love being, I am devoted. And I am inviting you to contemplate devotion for yourself. It starts with a simple question. To what or whom could you be devoted that would make this entire incarnation be worth it?

I invite you to come with me and discover the bliss of devotion. You may wish to study Mary Magdalene a bit, and ask her—yes, literally ask her—to be with you as you look to devotion. Devotion itself leaves nothing missing in our lives.

Yes, I do trust that devotion is only really to something sacred. One would never be "devoted" to evil. One could be attached to evil but never devoted. Devotion is reserved for the sacred.

Chapter 10

DAILY AFFIRMATION: SADHANA

Spiritual practice (sadhana) is the cultivation of divine love (prema).
—Sri Sathya Sai Baba

Some people find it difficult to start a meditation practice or daily sadhana (i.e., the Sanskrit term for a daily spiritual practice that involves surrendering the ego and connecting with universal energy). If you would like to have such a practice or expand your practice, let's try this together. It is very important to understand that there is no "place to get to." The point is not to be able to say "someday" I will be "awakened." Living with a "someday" goal is disempowering always, and especially in this matter. It is important to understand that in every split second you spend in a spiritual practice, you are awake in that split second. If you mediate for five minutes today, you have awakened yourself today! And, yes, there is a cumulative effect. But also, there is an immediate effect ... the very first minute you spend!

1. Establish a routine—the same 15 to 30 minutes each day at the same point in your routine (e.g., right after your shower).

2. Have a wonderful, comfortable place you love to sit. Make sure it is:
   a) A tranquil spot
   b) A lovely spot
   c) A comfortable place to sit (pillow on floor, great chair)—something with some back support
   d) A private place so you are not disturbed and so you are not self-conscious

3. Consider getting for yourself:
   a) An asana silk or wool meditation mat
   b) A picture of your favorite Divine Being (Christ, Sai Maa, Sai Baba, Gurumaye, Babaji, Mary Magdalene, or others)
   c) Incense
   d) A meditative playlist you love (check out Robert Gass's "Alleluia" and Ashana's "Ave Maria" and Christopher Duffley's "Open the Eyes of My Heart")
   e) Fresh flowers
   f) Mala beads

Let's start:
1) Light incense, place pictures and flowers where you want them
2) Be seated
3) Start with Sai Maa centering technique*
4) Select a mudra.* The most common is your hands resting palms up on the knees, with the index finger touching the palm of the thumb.
5) Chant 3–16 oms out loud
6) Repeat your chosen daily affirmation three times

Mine is:

**"I am devotion to Source,
I am Grace to all Creation"**

7) Stare in eyes of the divinity you have chosen, being aware of the prana that constitutes their divinity

8) Invite the divinity to come into your cells, your brain and breath, deeply inhaling their divine energy

9) Let the breathing relax

10) Play a guided meditation* if you have one you like, or simply be still; bring the awareness to the third eye

11) Imagine your day and imagine going to all your activities as light as love

12) When complete, express your gratitude to the Divinity for accompanying you on your journey

13) Be still until you are complete

Important note: Whatever happened, happened. There is no right experience or wrong experience to have. Just be aware of your experience, whatever it is.

*If you would like to experience Sai Maa's centering technique, you can search this title on YouTube: "How to Find Your Center with the Centering Technique."

To learn more about the mudras, visit this link: https://billharvey.org/mudra-book/.

And lastly, inside the companion course I have created a guided meditation that you can use for this practice if you desire.

Chapter 11

DIVINE LOVE

Divinity reveals herself in all things ... For she enfolds
and imparts herself even unto the smallest beings.
—Giordano Bruno

Can we wonder together what "divine love" might be?

Divine definition: "of, relating to or proceeding directly from God or a god."

In this writing, we are calling *divine love* the love that is proceeding directly from God.

So, can we, mere mortals, love divinely?

Good news again: *Yes, yes, yes,* we can!

You can offer anyone divine love.

I know. I know. You are not God. And yet. And yet. Does energy flow through you? Did you ever get a chill that shook your body?

Yes, I bet you have. So yes, energy flows through us.

Imagine now, my Beloved, that God's energy (prana) is everywhere in the universe, in every atom of every molecule of the universe.

Try this:

Close your eyes. Breathe naturally. Be still and quiet for a few moments.

Bring awareness to the universe surrounding you.

Start with the air that surrounds your body. Can you feel it on your cheeks, or the top of your head, or gently lying on your back and shoulders.

Let yourself experience the air all around you. Now imagine that every molecule of that air is alive with God's love. Can you feel it? No need to rush, take your time.

Your *Love* Does *Matter*

Again, start with the air that surrounds your body. Can you feel it on your cheeks, or the top of your head, or gently lying on your back and shoulders?

Now imagine every molecule of that air is filled with God's love (aka Source's love) for everything ever created.

Are you familiar with the movie *Ghost*?

In that movie, there is a scene where Whoopi Goldberg is playing the part of a spiritual medium, and in a very funny way, the spirits of the departed people she is channeling enter her body with a "whoosh" sound and take over her experience.

I have discovered that if I invite and welcome the energy of Jesus, or Mary Magdalene, Sai Maa, Sai Baba, and others to infuse my body, I can literally feel the energy enter my body and my soul. Yes, I speak out loud, my invitation: "Please come be with me, I invite you into me" and I speak out loud my welcome: "You are welcome here with me, in me."

I literally experience Mary's hands instead of my own, or Christ's heart where mine would be, or Maa's love in my DNA and emanating from my body to all that surrounds me. This experience is blissful.

But this book is not about spiritual bliss, it is about Love. So what is the point? The point is that when having such a blissful spiritual experience, love is pervasive and inescapable as a presence: any judgment, resentment, or opinion dissolves into love.

Love is permanent, which lets us discover that it is eternal. Resentments pass by like clouds in the sky ... but the sky is always there. Only that which is eternal is true. We are love, like the blue sky.

My chest gets filled with the whitest light; oftentimes I just naturally spread my arms in the air, embracing all of creation.

Divine Love

Welcoming the divine:

"Come to me, come to me," I say.

Now try this:

Invite that energy to come into the cells of your body.
Ask this energy to fill your heart.
Now ask this energy to fill your brain.
Now ask this energy to fill every cell of your hands.
Now ask this energy to fill every word you speak.

Imagine this energy flowing through your hands and activating every word you speak.

Now gently, gently touch a person or something in your environment (e.g., a pet, a plant, a photograph).

And imagine God's love for creation is flowing through your hands and blessing whoever/whatever you are touching.

Now say, "I love you."

Imagine this energy flowing into you and activating every word you speak.

Blessing, blessing, blessing whoever, whatever you are touching and speaking to.

This is what it means to love divinely. This is what it means to bestow Grace. The energy of God is what you are offering.

This all starts with your invitation to the energy of God. It is there. Where? Everywhere. When? Always. All you have to do is ask for it—invite it into every cell of you.

You could simply pray:

"Please fill every cell of my being with your vibrant love for all of creation."

Then offer your love. And trust that the love you are offering is activated. It is a blessing. You are the vehicle. Just ask: "Please flow through me. Please have my words and my hands heal all that needs to be healed with your love."

Yes, your love can be divine love. It requires simply that you invite God's love to come into you, move through you, and bathe all that you interact with. Go ahead. Ask now.

Enjoy.

Chapter 12

KNOWING YOURSELF AS SOMEONE WHO BESTOWS GRACE ON ANOTHER!

Grace is not part of consciousness; it is the amount of light in our souls, not knowledge nor reason.
—Pope Francis

In the historic paradigm, we relate to love as something that people either deserve or do not. We say things like, "They earned my love" or "They lost my love."

This is consistent with the teaching that the other person could have done something good or bad, and our loving them is dependent on them having done something "good." In previous chapters, I trust we have taken the wind out of the sails of any supposed value or validity of this moral context. As a reminder, it is absolutely impossible that anybody did anything wrong, precisely because there is no such thing as wrong in the world—wrong is a totally linguistic phenomena. In other words, we "say" things are right or wrong, good or bad—which doesn't make them that, it just makes them something we call that.

The consequence that breaks my heart for us (you) is that we end up withholding our love because we have some reason to, a reason based in a bankrupt paradigm!

But it we who that loves less, when all joy comes from loving.

So, could we not love everybody, at all times, no matter what ever happened? At first blush, you might say, "I don't want to love him/her!"

Pause, take a breath. Are you sure? How happy are you when you are loving? How happy are you when you are judging, condemning, or resenting?

Also, Love and relationship are two different things. You can love someone fully and not interact with them at all.

Would you be willing now to step out of the shackles of a moral paradigm and simply love? When? Now. Who? Everybody. Why? Because we can! And it gives us joy and peace and aliveness.

Grace sounds like this: "I love this person for no reason. My love does not have to be deserved, it is freely given. My love will never be taken away."

Yes, our love is infinite. Any limit to our love is unnatural and the result of some thought process we did not ask for and did not invent. Rather, it is a thought process we inherited from generations past—which has made it make sense to us to not love!

Does it make sense really? Think this through for yourself. If you got to educate all the young people today, would you teach them to stop loving under certain circumstances? Please do not confuse loving with being in a relationship. If you are in an abusive relationship, we beg you, *Get Out Now*! Get out of the relationship and keep love in your heart. Love and relationships are not the same *at all*!

With all of this said, can you bring to mind someone whom you have withheld love from? First notice the lack of joy you have even thinking about this person.

Now practice saying, "I give him/her my love, all my love ... for no reason. I will never ask them to deserve it, and I will never take it away. I bestow grace upon them."

Now enjoy—enjoy being someone who bestows grace on another.

Enjoy.

Chapter 13

Daring to Love Source Openly and Unabashedly: The Joy of Sharing with Sai Maa

Love Loves to Love Love.

—James Joyce

My Beloved reader: What follows are text messages I have sent to Sai Maa and Sai Maa's responses. As I have said, it is with Sai Maa that I recovered my freedom to love fully. That includes freely expressing my love to Sai Maa Herself.

I have included a favorite photo of Maa at the end of the book to share with you.

You may cut it out and bring her into your meditative practice if you wish.

I share these communications with you, so you can enjoy them like they are yours. Source loves all of us. Source loves you. Source's communications to me are Source's communications to All.

Please practice expressing your love, unabashedly, like I have in these messages.

Right now, who would you want to freely and unabashedly express your love for?

Is it a parent, a romantic interest, your child, a friend? Expressing your love freely and unabashedly is life giving, *really*!

*   *   *

Merry Christmas, Dear Maa
Infinite love and gratitude
Joy to the World

O my sweet sweet love, thank you for these blessings.
Blessings to you.
May Christ consciousness arise from within you in its splendor, totality and grace.
Ever yours, Maa

Om Jai Jai Sai Maa
I live to have Maa's love known by all
The way Maa loves lives so fully in my heart so I can share Maa's love
Everywhere with Everyone

Om Jai Jai Sai Maa
I am flooded with Maa
Eternally grateful for Maa having me remember my love of Master Jesus

My love of Baba
The ancient work we have done
The I Am Presence
From loving Maa, I know that as St Germain gifted us the violet flame I wish to gift all of humanity the joy of Grace

Om Jai Jai Sai Maa
Maa has always loved you
Maa will always love you
Maa loves you now eternally
Om Jai Jai Sai Maa my sweet one

Om Jai Jai Sai Maa
I am in awe of the sacred geometry
So beautiful
So perfect
So life giving
I am in awe

It is part of you sweetheart
Oh my dear love
You are loved by Grace
Om Jai Jai Sai Maa

Om Jai Jai Sai Maa
The love of Source is in every molecule of the Universe
Maa is everywhere
We are all Maa
Glory to Maa
Devotion to Sai Maa my Queen who is accompanying me in my
awakening
Thy will be done
I am Maa Maa is with me
No Boundaries

O you melt my sacred heart
Yes Yes Yes

My Love for Maa is greater than any love I have ever known
And the source of true bliss

With gratitude for the profound privilege of loving my Queen with all my soul

Absolutely.
It is so divine!!!

Om Jai Jai Sai Maa
I MISS MAA!!!
My eyes want to see Maa's beauty
My ears want to hear Maa's voice
My skin wants to feel the air move as Maa walks by
My nostrils want to smell Maa's glorious essence
My hands want to touch the earth Maa just stepped on
Oh I hunger to be physically with Maa with every breath I take
Om Jai Jai Sai Maa
My Love…
My Love…
My Love ….

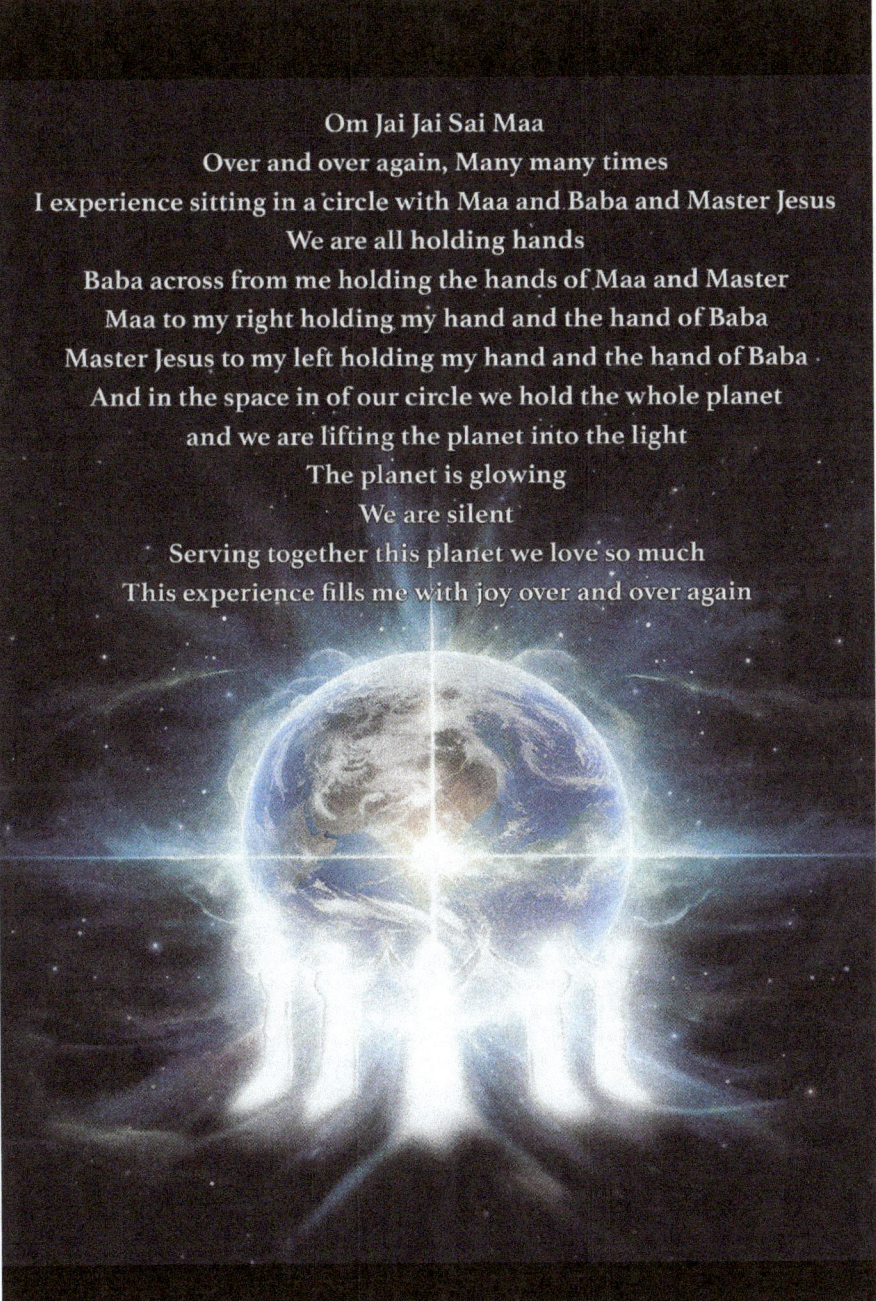

Om Jai Jai Sai Maa
Over and over again, Many many times
I experience sitting in a circle with Maa and Baba and Master Jesus
We are all holding hands
Baba across from me holding the hands of Maa and Master
Maa to my right holding my hand and the hand of Baba
Master Jesus to my left holding my hand and the hand of Baba
And in the space in of our circle we hold the whole planet
and we are lifting the planet into the light
The planet is glowing
We are silent
Serving together this planet we love so much
This experience fills me with joy over and over again

*A message I sent to Sai Maa which She had overlayed onto
this image she had created of the earth being held in Divine Love.*

Chapter 14

EVERYWHERE, ALL AT ONCE, ALL THE TIME (LOVING REMOTELY)

The chance to love and be loved exists
no matter where you are.
—Oprah Winfrey

Again, my grandchildren live in Connecticut, I live in Pennsylvania (a five-hour drive).

I always thought I had to be with them physically to express my love. Again, by the Grace of Sai Maa, I have learned to love them remotely!

We have been convinced we are our bodies and therefore are limited to a physical location. But if we are not the physical body, if we are light/love, then where do we exist?

Think about the light of the sun. Where is it? Isn't it wherever it is not blocked out? So, if we are light, where are we? Everywhere light is.

Is this light separate from that light? Look outside and see the light in front of your home. Now look at the light behind your home. Is it really a different light, or is it all just light?

So is the light where my grandchildren are separate from the light where I am, or is it all light, one light everywhere, all at once, all the time?!

And, it is completely real for me, as real as I am sitting at this desk typing right now, as light as love, I can be with them right now.

Yes, I literally experience being there, and my love is a substance that fills the room and wraps everybody in the experience of grace.

What if we can love remotely? What if we can heal remotely? What if our love is everywhere, all at once all the time? And since we are in love, we are everywhere, all at once all the time.

What is possible for humanity if we tap into that energy (possibility), if we harness that power?

Dear reader, think of someone you would love to love who is not with you physically. In your mind's eye, picture them where they are.

Imagine the room they are in. Picture their surroundings as vividly as you can.

Now imagine the light that wraps around them. Imagine activating that light, having it shine brighter.

Imagine them feeling that light on their face. Imagine that light wrapping around them ever so softly.

Again, fill the cells of the light with love. Activate the light so that it is emanating joyous, generous love.

Now, relate to the light as YOU! All that loving light is YOU!

Imagine that light giving them happiness.

Imagine that light healing them.

Imagine that light filling them with the experience of being peaceful.

Imagine them being happy to be them, loving themselves while you (light) are holding them.

Now, can you give up that this experience is not real? That only your physical existence in this body is you?

Maybe this is reality, and the separateness is an illusion!

I invite you to create this experience for yourself several times and see if it does not become more real each time.

Enjoy it. Practice loving political figures, children in the slums of Mumbai, women being domestically abused, anyone struggling with transitioning their gender, new mothers, the families of victims of gun violence, the police, and then anyone considered an enemy.

Can we stand for this making a real difference?!

Above I spoke about activating light energy. *Diksha* is a transference of Divine Light into the brain and nervous system, thus initiating the process of enlightenment. You may visit this link to further explore this pathway to new consciousness: https://awakenedlife.love/training-guidelines/

Chapter 15

HONORING OUR
WORD TO LOVE

Being deeply loved by someone gives you strength,
while loving someone deeply gives you courage.

—Lao Tzu

The first weekend that we spent together in 1983, Hayden got sick. Chuck, a physician friend of ours, said Hayden had pneumonia, but it was a strange kind of pneumonia that Chuck had never seen before.

In 1987, Hayden got sick again. The doctor said he had shingles, whooping cough, and scarlet fever!

A friend of mine asked me if I thought it could be AIDS. I was furious at the suggestion and said definitely, absolutely not.

Hayden disappeared one day. I was in Seattle, frantically calling home trying to find him. He was nowhere to be found.

Then I remembered that one day when he was upset Hayden had pointed out our living room window at the Chicago Hilton Hotel (a couple blocks away) and said to me, "I am going to move into the Hilton!"

From Seattle, I called the Hilton, asked for the manager, and told him that I was looking for Mr. Sealy. He said, "Oh, Mr. Sealy! Yes, he is here." He then let me know that Hayden had checked into the presidential suite for $2,000 a night, had bought all the men's clothes in the Lobby Shoppe, had already had two massages, and had ordered several hundred dollars of room service.

I was terrified, grief-stricken, and felt deep despair all at the same time. I remained as calm as I could. I asked him to let Hayden be for a little while longer and promised I would have my friend Sam be there ASAP to get him. I called Sam, and Sam jumped in to help. Sam arrived, knocked on the door of the room Hayden was in, and simply said, "Hayden, come with me."

Hayden did peacefully. Sam walked him to our doctor's office. Hayden walked in and collapsed in the doctor's arms.

The immediate diagnosis was that Hayden had had a psychotic break. He was placed in a psychiatric hospital. I flew home and went from the airport to the hospital. Hayden was in a secure room, stripped to underwear only. When he saw me he started to rant and rave about how he was being mistreated. It was impossible to speak with him. After a couple hours I knew I had to leave and leave him there! He begged me not to leave him, and the hardest moment of my life was to walk out that door and close it behind me.

I went to the park outside where there was a picnic table. I sat down and dealt with myself. I had promised, vowed, that I would never leave Hayden. And now, it looked like he would be in a mental institution forever. Was I going to honor my word and never leave him? Deep in my soul I found my answer. Yes, even if this was how it was for the next 100 years. I would honor my word to stay with him.

I discovered my integrity that day, which has been a foundation ever since. I discovered a depth to my love that gave me courage I did not know I had.

Hayden had not had a psychotic breakdown ... he did have AIDS. The AIDS virus was in his brain.

I realized the strange pneumonia he had the first weekend we were together was AIDS. He had AIDS from the minute we started being together. It still amazes me today that after all the exposure from Hayden I never was infected. Grace is the only explanation.

Chapter 16

WHO WE ARE *IS* LOVE!

*In the lotus of your heart God has put
the treasure of the Universe.*
—Her Holiness Jagadguru Sai Maa

If a person loses a limb, is the person still there? Yes, of course.

If the cells of a human body replicate themselves and the old cells are gone, is the person still there? Yes, of course.

So, actually, every cell of your body could be replaced, and you are still here?

Isn't the only obvious conclusion that we are not our bodies?

After we have a thought and it is gone, are we still here?

After we have an emotion and it is gone, are we still here?

Well then, if our thoughts and emotions can come and go and we still exist, isn't it the obvious conclusion that we are not our thoughts and emotions?

Could what people say about us change over time, and yet we continue to exist?

Could we stop doing something and still exist?

Could we find out for years that we have had a false memory of some life event and yet we still exist?

Isn't the only possible conclusion that we are not what is said about us, we are not our actions, and we are not our history?

Then who are we?

Dear reader, this is an important time to explore this question yourself. Sit with yourself; take the time to identify everything you think is you. Then do the work to discover for yourself that there is nothing that you are—in other words, you are no thing!

[The "Discovering I Am No Thing" audio-guide is in the companion course.]

Experience being *no thing*, and in a space of nothingness. This, my Beloved, is the space of creation. How does something get brought into existence from this sacred space? With language! Anything is brought into existence by speaking, period. So now, from nothing, you can speak yourself into existence. With the sacred saying, I am that I am _____. You can say anything.

I am inviting you to say, "I am that I am light, I am love!"

Then life is simple. Live the life of someone who said I am that I am light, I am love.

Chapter 17

THE POINT OF OTHER PEOPLE

To be brave is to love someone unconditionally,
without expecting anything in return.

—Madonna

Can you really look and see that other people cannot give you anything? If I love you and you are grumpy, will your life be filled with love or grumpiness? Try it out. If you love me and I am grumpy, will your life be filled with love or grumpiness? Again, try it out.

I cannot give you love, respect, or tenderness. If I respect you and you hate me, do you experience respect? The answer is no. If you respect me and I am rude, then do you experience respect? The answer is yes.

So, what does any other human being give us? The opportunity to *be* someone we love being, that is the one thing, and one thing only, another human being gives us.

Can you be loving if no one is there to love?

Can you be tender if there is no one to be tender with?

Can you be respectful if there is no one else there?

If you get this lesson, you will be on your knees grateful, for the presence of any other person in your life. And the worse they behave, the bigger we get to be.

A polite clerk in a store is an opportunity to be polite back.

A rude clerk in a store is an opportunity to be amazingly generous.

A great boss is an opportunity to be great back.

A difficult boss is an opportunity to be a really *big* person.

My husband of 30 years is named Bill.

The only time we get in trouble is when I think I am supposed to get something from him (e.g., love, acknowledgment)—forgetting he cannot give me anything except the opportunity to love him and be joyous as a loving husband. I am so grateful he is there, and I get to Love. If he was not there, I would not have that opportunity!

I would like to share with you more about my stepfather, Bob, who truly understood this principle of life, that other people provide us *one* thing only, which is the opportunity to be a human being we love being.

Bob was a man of traditional conservative values, and yet on the day that I took Hayden to Bob and my mom's home, he came to the car and picked Hayden up in his arms and took him inside. Hayden, a Black gay man with AIDS, couldn't have been more of a challenge to Bob's view of life, and yet he became for Bob the opportunity to be gracious, in fact Christ-like in his love. That's right; even someone you think is least like you, most foreign to your usual world, in fact gives you the opportunity to be most extraordinary with your love in the world.

Bob didn't miss this opportunity to be the human being he loved being, as challenging as the circumstances were.

I was 35 when this happened. Bob developed dementia when he was 77 and passed away at the age of 84, in February 2007. I never forgot the demonstration of love that Bob was for me, his wife, my mother, and most importantly for himself that day.

What does it take to see other people as our opportunity to be the human being we love being? *That view* of other people leaves us grateful for their presence in our lives, no matter who they are or how they are.

My son, my daughter-in-law, and my grandchildren all allow me to love them. Thank you, David, Jan, Garrett, and Lucas ... thank you for letting me love you.

I send them frequent texts expressing love in some way. They graciously accept them. My son and grandchildren let me hug them and kiss them even in public. See, they really are generous.

Chapter 18

FREEDOM FROM JUDGMENT

Out beyond ideas of wrongdoing and rightdoing,
There is a field. I'll meet you there.
When the soul lies down in that grass,
The world is too full to talk about.
Ideas, language, even the phrase each other
Doesn't make any sense.

—Rumi

Would you be willing to revisit the conversation we had in Chapter 5, regarding the nature of right/wrong, good/bad, and should/shouldn't?

Can you find anything that has been more worthless, indeed destructive to humanity than the concepts of right/wrong, good/bad, and should/shouldn't?

Think through for yourself the worth of these concepts.

Has telling someone that X is bad, had them not do it?

Telling someone it is wrong to use drugs, they shouldn't use drugs, drugs are bad—is there any evidence to suggest that is an effective deterrent?

Telling a child they should eat their vegetables—indeed vegetables are good for them—has that proven to be helpful, really?

Telling someone they should not speed in their car—has that been effective at all?

Think through for yourself the destructive nature of these concepts.

Every argument you have ever had, wasn't it one person saying X was right and the other person saying X is wrong?

Isn't all lack of self-love you may experience a function of a belief that something is wrong with you?

Hasn't the source of every war in the world been a disagreement over what is right and wrong?

Isn't all the vitriol in the current political conversation based on assertions of who and what is right and who or what is wrong, good, bad, and so on?

Now when you are present to the worthlessness and destructiveness of these concepts and then deal with the very nature of the concepts in the first place, look for yourself and see if you can find any good or bad in the world. Is there really any good music or bad music, or is there only music that we humans call good or bad?

Is the painting really good or bad, or do different critics have different opinions on the matter?

Is killing someone really bad? What about if you are protecting your home from a home invasion? What about in war? Would we say soldiers are bad for killing? What about capital punishment? The point is, is there any bad in the killing or is the bad *totally and completely* in what we say about the killing?

Yes, yes, yes, can we please acknowledge that the whole notion of good and bad exists not in the world, but only in our talking about the world? The existence of these concepts is 100 percent linguistic. They have no other existence except in talking.

We have forgotten we made it all up—not you and I, of course; we inherited these concepts and now we perpetuate them as if they are not made up.

It is one thing to say, "I am saying the music is bad" versus "The music is bad." It is one thing to say, "I am saying you are wrong" versus "You *are* wrong."

Now, if they served a purpose, fine. But do they?

What do you gain by saying the music is good or bad?

What else could you talk about?

Maybe, "What does this music provide?" or "How does this music make me feel?" or "Do I enjoy this music?"

Or, "The way I see this issue is X; I am curious about your view of the issue."

That's right. We each have a view of life. None of us have the same view. It would be impossible for us to have the same view of anything. Even if we put our cheeks side by side, we would still have a different view of whatever is in front of us.

Isn't it silly to argue which view is the right view? Couldn't we appreciate we have a view of any given situation, everyone else has their own view of any given situation, and **there is no such thing as a right view**!

So how could we powerfully relate to another's view, rather than argue with it if it is different than ours? There are so many ways:

    … be curious about their view
    … wonder what their view provides
    … discover why their view is important to them
    … acknowledge their view as a valid view

Now, can we please confront that until the concepts of right/ wrong, good/bad, and should/shouldn't disappear from our world- view? Individually and as a society we are trapped in judgment. We cannot escape being judgmental as long as we traffic in these con- cepts. And we cannot love as long as we are trapped in judgment. We cannot love others, we cannot love ourselves … it is only a matter of time until we find something *wrong* with them or us, and then the love we are is immediately contracted!

Could you join me in this movement? Read Chapter 23, "Love Goes to the Capitol," for just one possible example of how this would look.

I invite you to participate in The Love Matters Collaboration by visiting www.YourLoveDoesMatter.com or scanning the QR code found within this book.

Your Love Does Matter

Deepen your Work here.

SCAN
CODE

www.YourLoveDoesMatter.com

Chapter 19

Breaking from Source

Eskimo: "If I did not know about God and Sin, would I go to hell?"
Priest: "No, not if you did not know."
Eskimo: "Then why did you tell me?"
—Annie Dillard

God is love. I am love. I am God. The logic is inescapable.

But why do we not experience our own divinity?

When did we break our oneness with God?

Consider that we break our oneness with Source (e.g., God, parents, teachers, employers) whenever we do something we are sure Source does not want us to do.

After we do so, we have to make sources wrong (i.e., blame them) to justify our own behavior. We have to question their legitimacy as a source to allow ourselves to behave the way we do, especially if we are repeating the behavior.

Have you noticed adolescents start questioning God, even making God wrong?

Why is that? One clear-cut, obvious, and at the same time notably over-simplified explanation is that teenagers start being sexual. And given the moral code we have already discussed, most teenagers would believe that whatever they are doing sexually is bad, and therefore they themselves are bad.

In many faiths, you can notice the notion of sin is a fundamental tenet. In most faiths there is good and bad, and if you do something bad, that is a sin.

I just recently heard an evangelist on TV recommend starting all prayers with, "God, I am a sinner!"

Is that true?

Whether it is true or not, it is a fundamental belief of many faiths.

Again, please look for yourself and wonder if such a construct has been useful.

Has calling adultery a sin eliminated it from our culture? Obviously not. Does sin exist in the world, or it is a totally made-up construct? It may have been useful at some point in human history, but there is no evidence today that the title "sin" deters anybody's behavior (e.g., priests' sexual abuse of children). But if we take on the title "sinner," how can we relate to ourselves divinely? And if we cannot relate to ourselves divinely, then how are we supposed to love all people? And besides, they are sinners too!

What if none of this is true? What if it is all the erroneous conclusion of someone and then taught to the rest of us?

Have we done things we wish we had not done? I am certain.

Have we not done things we wish we had done? I am equally certain.

What makes any of it a "sin"? An obsolete and antiquated pedagogy.

But if we adhere to the whole notion of sin, then we will never be at one with God, with Source of any form. If we are not one with Source, we will not know our own love. God loves unconditionally. When you are free from the decision process that you are flawed, you love unconditionally. Notice that in everyday life. When you are whole with yourself, love is present. When you are down on yourself, love is never present.

Let's walk together into a new reality. All of us have done what we have done, and we have not done what we have not done. We never did something we did not do, and we never did not do something we did.

What did we do? What we did. What did we not do? What we did not do. When did we do it? When we did it.

How did we do it? The way we did it.

And in the absence of a story about it (e.g., it makes us a sinner), the event is over—period. End of paragraph. End of story.

God bestows grace on you. When? Now and eternally. Grace is ever present.

You are one with God. So now, bestow grace on every man, woman, and child walking the planet and be one with God/Source again.

It can be powerful to close the eyes and picture all of humanity in your mind's eye. Be still and hold humanity there in your mind's eye for at least a few moments. Imagine saying to all of humanity, "I wish you Peace. I wish you Health. I wish you Happiness. May you live in Grace."

SECTION 3

LIVING TODAY AND ESTABLISHING A NEW FOUNDATION FOR LIVING TOMORROW

Chapter 20

ACCEPTANCE

Happiness is a function of accepting what is.
—Werner Erhard

D ear reader, I think it is important you first explore what acceptance is not.

If we confuse acceptance with making something okay, approving of something, condoning that thing ... then we are back in the world of right/wrong, good/bad and should/shouldn't—ultimately the world of judgment (albeit judging something as okay).

Acceptance and judgment do not coexist; therefore, acceptance cannot be making something okay.

Well, if acceptance is not any kind of judgment at all, then what is it?

Then what is acceptance?

Consider that nothing is inherently okay or not okay.

Okay or not okay is only something we say about a thing—a label or description we impose in *our* speaking.

If we do not speak, then the thing is only and exactly what it is: neither okay or not okay, neither right or wrong, neither good or bad, neither a way it should be or shouldn't be. Again, without our speaking, anything is only and exactly what it is, period.

Aha! Acceptance is having something be exactly what it is and exactly what it is not? Imagine how effective we could become if we could deal with what something is versus deal with our judgment about it. For example, how effective could we be with a chronically late employee if we only dealt with the time of their arrival and not our judgment that they were a @#$%?

How much more effective are we when we are peaceful rather than when we are upset? Which gives peace, judgment or acceptance?

In one program I led, there were two people in particular that I remember interacting with. One man had recently contracted Bell's palsy. He was suffering, unable to accept this condition. I asked him if he believed that life without Bell's palsy was better than life with Bell's palsy. He was shocked by the question given to him. The answer was so obviously "YES, life without Bell's palsy would be a better life!" I asked him to really look to see if there was any such thing as "better" in the world, or is "better" a judgment we humans make about the world? At some point he saw it for himself, that "better" only exists in our speaking and consequent view of life and does not exist in life itself. In that moment, life with Bell's palsy and life without Bell's palsy became two distinct possible lives to live, not one better than the other. So, then I asked him, "Which life do you have?" He replied, "Life with Bell's palsy." The question is: How are you going to live that life, since that is the life you have? Without the illusion that there was a better life he should have, he could get busy living fully the life he actually had!

In the same program was a woman whose six-year-old son had died, five years earlier. She reported that since her son's death, she had closed her business, gotten a divorce, and was living a very isolated life. I gently asked the same question: "Is life with a son that lives better than life with a son who dies?" I was met with the same shocked response: "Of course life would be 'better' if my son had lived!" She courageously looked with me though to find where "better" existed and exhausted every pathway to find "better" in any circumstance of life and could only find "better" in what she was saying about life.

You could see the aha moment when she discovered that life with a son that lives and life with a son that dies are both possible lives a human being could have. The question is not "Which one is better?" Instead, the question is powerfully, "How do I live fully the life I actually have?"

We wept together as peacefulness descended upon her and she accepted the life she had.

My stepdad, Bob, was married to my mom for 30 years when he got severe dementia and forgot who my mom was. What my mom did every day for 5 years was stay at home and take care of Bob. She stopped going out with friends, she stopped even going to church. And while all of us would have begged for Bob not to have dementia, Bob did have dementia.

My mom did not suffer though. My mom thrived in that situation. My mom had discovered acceptance. One morning during breakfast, I watched Bob ask her at least 30 times, "What day is it?" I watched my mom answer, the 30th time no less patiently than the first, "It's Monday, Bob."

I then asked her, "Mom, how did you do that?!" Her reply was simple. "Well," she said, "I wished he asked me a different question.

But if I wait for the question I want, I don't get to talk to my husband. If I answer the question he asks me, at least for a moment I get to talk to my husband. I'll answer any question he asks me; I don't care how many times." That is acceptance. With acceptance comes peace. With peace comes effective action.

My Beautiful Mother.

Do not worry. Acceptance does not breed complacency. Defeat breeds complacency. Acceptance breeds effective action.

Dear reader, I wish you peace and effectiveness. The pathway is acceptance. It's so much easier than judgment.

Enjoy accepting! Accepting what? Everything about you, others, and life itself!

Acceptance is a very high state of being. Enjoy.

Chapter 21

FORGIVING

Forgiveness is the fragrance that the violet
sheds on the heel that has crushed it.
—Mark Twain

Forgiveness—can we love fully without forgiveness?

At this point in our evolution, we have not freed ourselves from judgments, resentment, and anger, have we? Aren't judgment, resentment, and anger still frequent, if not almost constant experiences for most of us?

Now, we may not notice how common the experiences of judgment, resentment, or anger are because the more common something is, the less we notice it.

Can we courageously bring our awareness to these experiences and resist letting them disappear into a fog of commonness? I invite you to stop now and take notice of the frequency of these experiences for yourself. It would be helpful to remember actual occasions where you experienced judgment, resentment, or anger in the last two days. Did you? When and with whom, or about what?

Therefore, without forgiveness—that is to say, without freeing ourselves from these experiences of judgment, resentment, and anger—can we love fully?

Don't we have to acknowledge that resentment and love do not coexist at the same time? In any moment of time, wouldn't we be either resenting or loving, but not both at the same time?

So, if we take the case that we will never love fully without forgiveness, then don't we each need to resolve that there is nothing we cannot forgive?

My friend Earl (with whom I co-lead a support group in a halfway house for men right out of prison) had his right leg amputated after being shot 28 times in that one leg.

The man who shot Earl had been lied to and therefore shot Earl based on misinformation. Earl has fully forgiven the man who shot him and the man that lied to the man that shot him.

If Earl can forgive those two men, is there anybody who cannot be forgiven?

I appreciate, my Beloved reader, that you may find it difficult to imagine such forgiveness or to have such forgiveness make sense to you.

Finding such forgiveness difficult and illogical is inevitable inside of everything you and I have been taught and the language we inherited that has us see resentment as logical, merited, and valuable rather than the poison it is. (Resentment: the poison we give ourselves hoping the other person dies.)

In the next few paragraphs, I have tried to reframe forgiveness in a way that makes forgiveness both accessible and compelling.

The next few paragraphs set you free from the burden and suffering of resenting.

Come with me and let's discover the freedom, power, and joy of forgiveness together.

Can you imagine a life resenting nothing and no one? How peaceful and fulfilling could that be. That is the gift of this chapter—for you!

Most people (and remember, my Beloved, that is a group we all belong to) think forgiveness sounds like this: "I forgive you for being such a jerk!"

Most people think you have to "feel" forgiveness before you can forgive authentically.

Most people think forgiveness has to make sense to you before you can forgive authentically.

Most people worry that when you forgive you condone what happened, or at least let the perpetrator "off the hook."

All of this is an old paradigm that stops you from loving, that stops the flow and expression of the love you are.

Dear reader:

What if forgiveness starts with a speech act, starting with saying the words "I forgive"?

What if what we were communicating is this:

1) "When X happened, I took away my love and started resenting you."
2) "I give up resenting you, and I give you back my love, like I did before anything happened."

That's it—that simple and straightforward.

Fore/Give: I give my love to you like I did before (anything happened).

That is our power. We have the power to love no matter who, when, where ... don't we?

They might be able to put us in jail and hold a gun to our head, but they cannot stop us from loving, can they?

What if forgiveness does not have to make sense? What if you don't have to feel any certain way to forgive? Remember, my Beloveds, love is a way of *being*.

You invent (create) yourself in your speaking as someone who loves, then you step back into life and take actions a loving person would take, **and then** have the experience and feelings a loving person has.

So integrity is then simple: I live the life of somebody who says "I forgive."

Could you practice that now? Is there someone you have been resenting (either another or yourself)?

Practice saying to that person: "I took my love away from you. I give it back now."

They may ask, "Why? When?"

You can ask them to let you not answer that question because it really does not matter. If they insist on an answer you can tell them what happened, making the point very clear that you are not blaming what happened for anything ... you are taking full responsibility that no matter what happened it was you who took your love away and therefore (ready for the good news?) it is you who can give your love back! You don't have to. It may not even make sense.

So why forgive?

Get present to your experience of life when you are resenting. What is it like to live life resenting?

Now, get present to living a forgiving, loving life. What is it to like to live life loving and forgiving?

You see, forgiveness isn't for them. I mean, they may enjoy being forgiven; that is accurate. But, what about you? You hate resenting, don't you? You suffer when you are resentful, don't you? You are at peace when you are forgiving, are you not? You are happy to be you when you are forgiving, are you not?

Isn't resenting burdensome and tiring and lonesome?

Isn't loving nourishing, peaceful, and joyful?

Okay, it is your life. Resent or "for-give." Choose.

You can live either life; it is totally up to you.

Choose now. Which one do you choose?

Let's choose love.

When? Always.

With whom? Everyone (including ourselves).

Why? Because we can and it enlivens us.

As I write this chapter, it is the second anniversary of the Uvalde school shooting in Texas. I am not arrogant enough to think that I know what it is to be the family of one of those killed in that school that day. I can try to imagine their grief, their anger, their helplessness—but it is ultimately their experience, not mine.

And what I want for them with every ounce of my being is that they find their power to forgive the boy who murdered their loved ones.

Why? Certainly not for moral reasons (i.e., the right thing, the good thing to do is forgive). Not at all; that would be absurd to propose.

And if I imagine the life of any one of those family members that resents the murderer, wishes harm for the murderer, I fear their suffering.

And if I imagine the life of any one of those family members who holds the murderer compassionately in the love and light of their heart, loving him as a choice—choosing loving over resenting—I am not worried about their suffering.

Of course they will grieve, as much as anyone has ever grieved.

On Grief

We must be aware that grieving and suffering are not the same. Grieving and suffering are indeed two very different phenomena. Suffering only comes into play when we make grieving wrong (i.e., "I should not be grieving" or "Grieving is horrible"). If we have grieving be grieving—if we accept grieving—then we will grieve but not suffer. I found when my Hayden died, at first I resented grieving and suffered while I was grieving. At some point, I embraced the grieving, and the grieving became an expression of my love for Hayden, and I no longer suffered; I only grieved.

Also, sometimes forgiveness requires humility. When someone else does something we often say, "I would never do that," or "If I were in their shoes …"

But the point is not if we were in their shoes. The point is if we were *them* in their shoes. What if we were them? What if we had had their life, their experiences? What if we had been through what they had been through (and we never know fully what another has been through, do we?)? What if we had their body, their teachers, their thoughts? Do we really think we would have behaved differently? At best, we must confess that we do not know for sure.

We might have handled their life differently, but we are not them. If we were them, would we have handled our life differently? If we can acknowledge that we cannot be sure, any arrogance that would prohibit forgiveness can disappear and forgiveness is once again possible.

My Beloveds: Forgiveness is for you, not for the one being forgiven. It nurtures you, it comforts you, it releases you from the suffering that goes along with resenting.

If you remain concerned that your forgiveness condones what was done, you can say, "I am giving up resenting you, I forgive you … I will never condone what you did, and I will not resent you for it. I give you my love back like I did before anything happened."

Don't worry if it makes sense.

Don't worry if you feel like it.

Say it and then simply set about living the life of one who said, "I forgive."

I will always wish you forgiveness as a way of being.

Martin Luther King: "We must develop and maintain the capacity to forgive. He who is devoid of the power to forgive is devoid of the power to love."

And what I would add is that he who is devoid of the awareness that there is **no *such thing*** as right/wrong and good/bad is devoid of the power to forgive.

Chapter 22

BETTING IT ALL ON YOUR LOVE

*Have enough courage to trust love one
more time and always one more time.*

—Maya Angelou

My Beloveds: Ask yourself, what do you rely on to have everything you want to have happen, happen? What do you want to have happen?

I want:

My kids to do their homework
My boss to give me a promotion
My neighbors to control their dog
My neighbors to stop making so much noise
My congressperson to listen to me
To make more money
To lose weight
To finish my book
To talk politics in a calm way with my dad
To stop arguing with my mom

To _____ (whatever you want)

Now, what do you rely on to make everything above happen?
Being right?
Being logical?
Being forceful?
Being convincing?
Being secretive?
Being attractive?
Bullying?
Lying?
Staying away?
Shutting up?
Pretending?

We got trapped, didn't we?

We got roped into a paradigm that one thing is right and another thing is wrong, one thing is good and another thing is bad, one thing should be and another thing should not be. Don't we try to accomplish everything by being right, or at least insisting we are right?

We have already examined both the absurdity and the utter bankruptcy of that paradigm.

It takes courage, real courage, to give up relying on being right.

Aren't we afraid to rely only on our love?

But what if, in the face of any challenge with another person, we relied on loving them, forgiving them, blessing them, bestowing Grace upon them as our pathway to resolving any difficulty between us? What if instead of turning to righteousness and domination, force, convincing, or manipulation—what if we turned only to compassion and love? What if we all did so, and that became inherent to our new lifestyle? Could we take this journey together?

So, for example, imagine being trapped in thinking your daughter-in-law is parenting wrongly. Rather than correct her, gossip about her, keep distance between you, try something radical: love her, bless her, bestow Grace upon her.

That's right, take her into your heart and hold her preciously there and then see if you can't work everything out together.

Or imagine being trapped in believing your neighbor is a problem because they play their music too loud. What would be normal is to complain about them and gossip about them to others. What would be normal is to righteously demand they "turn the music down!" What would be normal is to be cold and distant in interactions with them and avoid them.

What if instead we turned only to love and with full love, respect, and acceptance talked with them about what they want and what we want and how we could work any conflict out together, as loving neighbors?!

What does it look like to be committed to "rely on love"?

Where to look is any area of life where you struggle or are less than satisfied, especially in a relationship. Note: All areas of life actually function in relationship with others. So if you are struggling with a project, reflect on the people involved and the nature of your relationship with those people.

Once having identified the area of life or the person involved, ask yourself, "What am I relying on to resolve this situation or relationship?" I invite you to consider that some of what you might be relying on is being right, logical, convincing, forceful, authoritative, strategic, secretive, attractive, dominant, and the like.

Notice, it is not working, *and* it is not satisfying.

What else could you rely on? What if you relied totally on your Love? What will give you the power to resolve anything with anybody is giving them all your love … taking them in your arms and loving them. You cannot really dance with someone who is not in your arms, can you?

If there is something that stops you from loving fully (e.g., fear, righteousness, etc.) what works is to acknowledge such, accept such, set it aside and let it be, without trying to fix it or change it—let it be. Imagine putting a set of keys down on a table and walking away and leaving them there. Would you be willing to do that with any judgment, resentment, righteousness, or anger that you are holding onto for another? Would you be willing to lay it down and walk away from it? You don't have to get rid of it. You can lay it down.

Would you try that now? It may sound too simple, so try it now. Take something (keys or any other object) and experience holding on to it. Now place the object down on a table or counter and walk away from it. You can do that, can you not? You did not have to change it or get rid of it, did you? We often think we have to change our opinions of people. Actually, no; we can just lay our opinions down without changing them. Now go back and pick the object up again. You can do that as well, can you not, at any time? You can pick an opinion back up at any time as well, not to worry.

And when you lay them down, you are free.

In the freedom that ensues, let yourself love. Your love will flow naturally when you are free from fear and free from righteousness.

Imagine taking the person in your arms. Imagine pulling them to your heart. Imagine embracing them. Now imagine being with them and resolving everything, *all* of it, with your love.

How to Practice Relying on Your Love

1. Identify a person you are struggling with.
2. Ask yourself, "What am I relying on?" (being right, convincing, strategic, dominant, etc.)
3. Ask yourself, "What's in the way of me relying on love?" (fear, anger, judgment, etc.)
4. Don't resist it, don't fix it, don't get rid of it. Let it be there. Put it aside. Walk away from it.
5. Bring the person to your heart.
6. Place them in your arms.
7. Bring resolution with them from Love.

May your Love prevail!

Chapter 23

LOVE GOES TO THE CAPITOL

We realize the importance of our voices
only when we are silenced.
—Malala Yousafzai

I ran for political office in 2022. I was encouraged to run when a candidate dropped out of the race two months before election day. So I had two months to campaign. I was up against a six-term incumbent whose party had a 70 percent majority in the district.

I had been committed that if, by a long chance, I did win, I would alter the culture of state politics, bringing unprecedented respect and love to the discourse. I was expected to get 18 percent of the vote and got 41 percent!

It was overall a great experience. I was encouraged to run again but said no.

I made a new vow to myself that I would never put myself in a position of having to say "no" to anything Sai Maa asked me to do.

In previous years, Sai Maa had asked me to do things (e.g., go to Japan for her) and I felt obliged to say no because of work obligations. So I now vowed I would never put myself in that position again and therefore said no to running for office.

In saying no, however, I was bothered that I would not make a difference with the culture, which can fairly be described as fear-based and full of vitriol.

How I resolved that is by starting a new project called "Love Goes to the Capitol." The idea is simple. Have a group of formerly incarcerated men go to the Capitol and deliver orchids to every legislator. And have a group of transgender teenagers go to the Capitol and simply open doors graciously for everyone arriving in the morning.

No political talk, just pure expressions of love, honor, and acknowledgment. Then keep this up, with ideas like this until Love wins. The environment is one of honor, love, grace.

I am writing this at the time of an assassination attempt on Donald Trump, in July 2024.

The pundits are all saying, "We have to tone down the rhetoric." Yes, that is essential. And it is not enough. The divisiveness that people are saying needs to be disappeared is a function of the paradigm of right and wrong that remains pervasive and unexamined, and a lack of insight into any view of life being *a* view of life and impossible to be the right view of life.

I am starting the Love Goes to the Capitol project in Pennsylvania, and I am planning to have this become a national movement, and then even spread to other countries. I am sure people around the United States could come up with hundreds of ideas that cost nothing and infuse the political environment with the energy of Love.

Do you have any ideas for simple actions like those above that would infuse the environment of your state capitol with Love? How about a gracious thank-you note to every legislator, thanking them for being a legislator no matter how they vote on any topic? Or how about music performances at the capitol building that communicate Love? Or maybe just banners in or around the capitol building that evoke love and respect of all people? Maybe a lapel ribbon each legislator wears symbolizing Love Matters? Maybe a very humanizing short bio of each legislator that leaves everyone appreciating their humanity in a deeper way? Please, my Beloved, do not be limited by these suggestions. Trust yours and others' heart-based creativity—let's share ideas and start a movement!

If you would like to create something in this movement, please go to www.YourLoveDoesMatter.com. There you will have the opportunity to find out more and participate, if you would like to, in the Love Goes to the Capitol movement.

Chapter 24

SELF-LOVE

Love yourself first and everything else falls into line.
—Lucille Ball

Throughout this journey, we have focused on loving outwardly (i.e., loving others).

Now let's talk about loving inwardly (i.e., loving yourself).

Wasn't there a time before you had any judgments of yourself? Wasn't there a time before you thought anything at all was wrong with you? I promise you there was. As we talked about earlier, it was before you acquired language. Didn't you have to learn the word *wrong* before anything could be wrong with you? Yes, of course.

So now, would you give the whole notion that something can be wrong with a person back to the people who made it up—and reclaim *you* exactly the way you are and exactly the way you are not? And right now, before we complete this journey together, would you give your love back to yourself? There was a time before you were taught something could be, and in fact was, wrong with you. Give that lesson back to the teachers of it and let them know you decline to abide by it. Let them know you have chosen the path of acceptance and forgiveness toward all—and that includes you!

You do not have to convince yourself nothing is wrong with you; that is a mistake people make. Remember, it is impossible that anything is wrong with you, because there is no such thing! (I know, I know, that means there is nothing right about you either; sorry, that would be made up too!)

You are the way you are, and you are not the way you are not—period, end of story!

Do you love the light, God, Source, whatever you wish to name it? Do you love Love?

Yes, I know you do. And are you light?

Look at the natural light around you. It comes from the sun, does it not? Now ask yourself: Is it disconnected from the sun, or is it simply a ray of the sun that is continuous and unbroken? Indeed, the sun is shining where you are and is not a chunk of sunlight somehow broken off and fallen. I understand you are living here on Earth—and not in heaven. Like the sunshine, you are not broken off and fallen. Please see for yourself that you are a continuous and unbroken ray of God, Light, Love that is God, shining here. If you love God, if you love the light, if you love Love, then you must love yourself because that is precisely who you are!

Look outside where the sun is shining. See it nurture the leaves of the trees, the blades of grass. Notice all life happens in this light. Let yourself experience gratitude for this light. Let yourself experience love for this light.

Now, close your eyes. Be still. Focus on the heart area. See the light that is there. Let yourself experience gratitude for this light. Let yourself experience love for this light. Now, be struck again by the awareness that that light is you ... that is who you are. Say out loud: "I am the light. I love the light. I love who I am. I love mySELF!"

Enjoy!

Chapter 25

FELLOW TRAVELERS (GOING FIRST)

*Deep within, you know that the only thing that
really matters is being in alignment with spirit.*
—Wayne Dyer

My Beloveds, in the introduction to his book I invited us to be fellow travelers on this journey to a new consciousness.

Well, we are packed and ready to go! So what is our destination?

Can you imagine it is really possible for us to have Love prevail on the planet? Do you think we can have Love be pervasive?

What if Love prevailed in all the situations we are dealing with?

I am writing this in 2024. I just saw on the news a group of young women athletes protesting against trans women being able to participate in women's sports. None of us know exactly what to do about this situation. How do we give trans women an opportunity to compete athletically and at the same time protect cisgender women's right to fair competition? It is really a quandary. Here is what is striking though. The protests were filled with resentment, judgment, anger, and accusations. As I watched, I wondered, "Where is the love?" One young woman said, "A man pretending to be a woman has no right to compete with us."

Okay. But first of all, no trans woman would say she was pretending to be a woman; a trans woman would say, "I am a woman."

But even putting that aside, where is the love? Couldn't this be framed inside of "I love you, let's work this out together"?

What would that take?

Yes, it would take stepping outside of the paradigm of right and wrong, should and shouldn't, fair and unfair (remember Chapter 5?).

Yes, it would take stepping out of the illusion that you are not me and I am not you (again Chapter 5) And then, *and only then*, what comes naturally is:

Yes, it would take simply wishing one another well—simple, isn't it? Simply wishing one another well.

Yes, it would take bestowing Grace.

It has become normal to hate, judge, scorn, and wish harm to others. Hate, judgment, scorn, and wishing harm to others only happens because of the illusion that there are others! Because something becomes normal, that does not mean it is natural, does it? Isn't love natural to us?

Look at an infant cuddle naturally—do you see any judgment, scorn, or hate there? Didn't we learn to judge after we learned language? Doesn't it take language to judge (i.e., "He is so *XXX*" or "She is so *XXX*"). Aren't judgments totally made up?

Can anything that is totally made up be true?

What if we didn't wait for anybody else to be kind? What if we didn't wait for anybody else to bestow Grace? What if we didn't wait for anybody else to forgive? What if we didn't wait for anybody else to apologize? What if we didn't wait for anybody else to wish another well?

What if we just always were willing to go first? (I know, I know, we were taught that there is something called fair and unfair and that is not fair!) Can't we now learn that the whole notion of fair and unfair is made up—in reality, nothing is fair and nothing is un-fair—everything is just what it is? What if we never worried again about whether something is fair or not? What if we only worried if everyone is experiencing being loved?

Out of my love for you, I want you to never question again that your love *does* matter. Every ounce of love that you put into the world is difference-making for all of humanity. How you love and who you love is yours to choose.

So, Fellow Travelers, I love you. Let's accompany one another on this journey now. Your love does matter, so does mine, so does everyone's. Let the energy of Divine Love awaken in your cells, in your DNA, and let your brain illuminate with Love energy of Source and let your heart soften and embrace all that is.

Be still.
Be still.
Be still.

Experience the love of Source (prana) that is there in the stillness knowing it is you … and say, "I am perfect, endless love for all of cre-ation." Experience the peace that goes with that declaration. Love loving. Together, we will have Love prevail.

End.

AFTERWORD

And in the end, the love you take is
equal to the love you make.
—Paul McCartney and John Lennon,
The Beatles, 1969

During the final weeks of writing Your *Love* Does *Matter*, I suffered a mild stroke.

Although I was blessed to have no permanent damage, the event itself was quite an upheaval. I was in California, not Pennsylvania where I live, and had to be hospitalized twice while in Los Angeles.

Upon discharge from the hospital, I was instructed not to fly, and my husband, Bill, flew to gather me up and we drove five days all the way home. Once home, I had to alter my lifestyle and include physical therapy and other blood treatments. After returning home, I had one other incident and had to be taken by ambulance to the local hospital to stabilize my blood pressure.

There were three vivid lessons I learned during this whole time:

First: There is no circumstance under which we cannot generate Love, and in which our love does not make a difference. The hospital staff were undauntable heroes, and it was wonderful to watch them be refreshed instantly in their humanity as I loved them fully.

At one point I was on a gurney, in a chaotic and crowded hallway, where the nurses were constantly challenged by the sheer volume of demand upon them. I remember vividly the smile that would soften their strained faces when I looked them in the eye and simply thanked them with all my heart. More than once, their eyes welled up with tears at being seen and known and appreciated. Again, I learned our love does matter, everywhere, all the time.

Second: It is so empowering to be present to your purpose for living, even if we are not sure exactly what that purpose is … simply being aware we must have one.

Sai Maa was very attentive to my care and progress. As I grappled with having someone of such consequence for the world attending to my personal care, the only possible conclusion was I must be here (on earth, this lifetime) for a reason; I must have some contribution to make to the planet. She is not doing all this so I can get well and goof off. I was affirmed in resolving I am here *to have love prevail as the preeminent way of being on the planet.* That is my purpose. It is ridiculously empowering to be present to purposeful living.

Third, and the real point of this afterword:

As important as it is to generate love, it matters to receive the love of others as well.

During this time, I was on the receiving end of an outpouring of generous, gracious love. Call after call, offer after offer, prayer after prayer—the gifts were constant and selfless. Truthfully, at first, I found myself embarrassed to receive such tender blessings. And I somehow knew that my accepting all these expressions of love was important for two reasons: It was healing for me and it was life giving to them. Sometimes I would just close my eyes and let the love wrap around me, and I swear the cells of my body were energized immediately. My worries would dissolve, and my heart would be full.

And as I welcomed and accepted any expression of love from another, the other person would immediately say something like, "Okay, all is well, everything is going to be okay," and peace and serenity would descend upon them.

Sai Maa once taught me that when someone expresses love to us, we often send it back with the statement, "I love you too!" Sai Maa recommended, "It is wonderful to be loved by you!" as a new response that allows you to fully receive the love and allows the other to be fully satisfied that their love was received and welcomed.

So, my Beloved, your love of the love that is expressed to you matters as much as the love you generate for others. Together, let's welcome Love. Let's honor Love. Let's praise Love. Let's cherish Love in all forms and directions. Together, we will bring forth new consciousness and a planet where Love prevails as the preeminent way of being.

With all my love, I hold you in the most precious place in my heart,

David

If you would like to participate further with David in any of his programs or initiatives, please scan the QR code below. You will also find a companion course to this book that will support you to deepen the practices and lessons shared here.

Your Love
Does Matter

Deepen your Work here.

SCAN
CODE

www.YourLoveDoesMatter.com

Prayer of Grace

May I use these arms to hold the world tenderly
May I use these hands to heal all who suffer
May I use these eyes to see the divine within all people
May I use these ears to listen for the truth
May I use this mind to think of us as light beings
May I use this mouth to create possibility, remembrance, awareness and devotion and creation itself
May I use these feet to walk in the world and bestow grace on all
May I use this heart to love without conditions
May I use this whole being to anchor the dimension of love on this planet

💛💜💛💜💛💜💛💜

David Cunningham

My Beloved, this photograph is a gift from me to you of Her Holiness Sai Maa, so that you also have Her presence and energy in your home.

Love,

David